TEACHING
VISUAL CULTURE

TEACHING VISUAL CULTURE

Curriculum, Aesthetics and the Social Life of Art

KERRY FREEDMAN

Teachers College, Columbia University
New York and London

National Art Education
Association

Published simultaneously by Teachers College Press, 1234 Amsterdam Avenue, New York, NY 10027, and the National Art Education Association, 1916 Association Drive, Reston, VA 20191-1590

Copyright © 2003 by Teachers College, Columbia University

Library of Congress Cataloging-in-Publication Data

Freedman, Kerry.
    Teaching visual culture : curriculum, aesthetics, and the social life of art / Kerry Freedman.
      p. cm.
    Includes bibliographical references and index.
    ISBN 0-8077-4372-0 (cloth : alk. paper) — ISBN 0-8077-4371-2 (pbk. : alk. paper)
    1. Art—Study and teaching.   2. Art—Philosophy.   I. Title.

N84.F74 2003
707'.1—dc21   2003050406

ISBN 0-8077-4371-2 (paper)
ISBN 0-8077-4372-0 (cloth)

Printed on acid-free paper

Manufactured in the United States of America

10   09   8   7   6   5   4   3

This book is dedicated to the next generation of my family:

Chris, Kara, and Jay

Caitlin, Liz, Gandy, Maggie, Rob, Kati, Anthony, and Devin

Contents

Acknowledgments

I WISH TO THANK THE MANY PEOPLE who have supported me in this project. Special thanks go to Brian Ellerbeck and the other folks at Teachers College Press who have provided guidance in the completion of the book. My work on this project was done while on the faculty at University of Minnesota and Northern Illinois University and I thank both institutions for their support.

Several colleagues who have read all or parts of the manuscript have given me helpful advice and deserve special mention: Paul Duncum, Arthur Efland, Patricia Stuhr, Deborah Smith-Shank, and Kevin Tavin. Thanks to Karen Schuler and Mei-Ioc Chan who helped with referencing, editing, and indexing and to the students who have enabled the idea of this book to be realized in practice. Finally, I am most grateful to my husband and colleague, Doug Boughton, whose inspiration and understanding helps to keep me aloft.

Introduction

THIS BOOK IS ABOUT THE INTERSECTION OF ART AND education at all levels. In a sense, art is an education. Art is communicative and can help people understand aspects of the world that they could not gain access to through other means. A work of visual art can even teach people how to look at itself superficially. Many examples of the visual arts have surface qualities that are understandable without the need for formal instruction. Those visual qualities that interact with our biological processing systems to enable humans to live in and adapt to new visual environments have enabled us to survive since early human history, and now allow us to process realistic imagery quickly. Even young children can interpret those surface visual qualities. However, those visual qualities are not what define visual forms as works of art and culture. It is not the fact that we can see and interpret basic forms that makes them worthy of academic study. Rather, it is the amazing human capability that enables people to make images and objects that other people want to look at, create meaning from, and come to value. Although the potential for making things is "hardwired" into our brains, the skills and concepts needed for creating, understanding, valuing, and critiquing the visual arts are learned.

The process of learning to make and adequately respond to the complexities of the visual arts is unlikely to occur without guidance. Unless people are given instruction, they may never get beyond the surface of the images and designed objects they see every day. When students develop a deeper understanding of their visual experiences, they can look critically at surface appearances and begin to reflect on the importance of the visual arts in shaping culture, society, and even individual identity. Unfortunately, most people have no formal art education after early adolescence and many have no instruction in the visual arts at all.

Insufficient art education is a concern not only because the visual arts have been historically important, or because the visual arts are important as forms of human expression, but because much contemporary culture has become visual. Global culture is rapidly shifting from text-based communication to image saturation. Visual culture is seen on television, in museums, in magazines, in movie theaters, on billboards, on computers, in shopping malls and so on, and the evidence of its influences is overwhelming. As a result, learning about the complexities of visual culture is becoming ever more critical to human development, necessitating changes in conceptions of art and education.

This book is about what is taught by visual culture and what should be taught about it in a contemporary democracy and as part of global culture. The book is organized into two parts. The first half focuses on theorizing art in education. Theory provides a foundation and rationale for practice as well as being constructed through practice. An area of study such as art education requires a social form of theory in which principles both guide and challenge practice.

Theorizing art in education is difficult because it involves two often conflicting forms of practice—education, which seeks predicted learning outcomes; and art, which seeks the unpredictable. However, the potential contribution of theory in art education is far-reaching, making the overt and serious consideration of theory critically important. Historically, theory has been crucial to the fine art community as a way of helping people think and talk about the arts. Theory is becoming increasingly important in terms of broader visual culture as technology has made the influence of imagery more palpable. In the last century, educational theory, often based on empirical research, has increasingly influenced practice, as indeed practice influences theory. With two such theory-rich foundation areas of inquiry, art education seems undertheorized in the sense that curriculum is often a succession of isolated, skill-based activities rather than being based on rich conceptual frameworks. Although the institutional limitations of art education contexts will always work to confound the enriching influence of theory, the struggle of theorizing must continue to sustain the professional field for the benefit of students.

In the first chapter, I discuss art education as a professional field that influences all levels of education and as a form of social production tied to larger symbolic practices of visual culture. Visual culture creates, as well as reflects, personal and social freedoms, and as a result, consideration of its character and impact is critical to a democratic education. As such, how and what people come to know about art, inside and outside of institutions, is important in the formation of cultural identity, political economy, and individual enrichment.

The discussion of theory continues in Chapter 2, but shifts to a focus on aesthetics in curriculum. This chapter includes a reconsideration of theories concerning the relationship between form and content in the visual arts and art instruction. Contemporary art curriculum must address issues of postmodern aesthetics, but this is difficult in the context of resilient modernistic institutional structures. Educators' responses to such conflicts will shape the future of art education at all levels. Curriculum is an artistic form that borrows from scientific inquiry, but an aesthetic education can aid understanding of what the science of teaching overlooks. As a result, the neopragmatism of postmodern aesthetics is an aesthetic for art education.

Philosophical and historical foundations of the visual arts and education are important to teaching visual culture. Some philosophical foundations are discussed in Chapter 2; historical foundations are presented in Chapter 3, which also addresses some recent changes in the field of art history and other postmodern conditions of the academy. From an educational perspective, it is important to remember that history is not the past—it is a *story* about the past. At all levels of education in the past, that story has been largely Western and represented as a history of styles, barely touching on the most important social and cultural issues of art. The importance of social considerations, both of makers and viewers, has been largely neglected in art education in the face of social interpretations continually being carried along in people's minds, images, and texts. As a result, a social history of visual culture can be considered a more enriching educational representation of art.

Chapter 4 is about connections between art, student development, and cognition. This chapter brings together research on the relationship between perception and meaning in the cognitive processing of art, of distributed cognition, and constructivist learning theory. These perspectives of learning maintain social aspects of cognition at their center and therefore can be important contributions to an understanding of teaching and learning about visual culture.

The second half of the book draws on the theory discussed in the earlier chapters toward putting ideas into practice. In Chapter 5, I discuss interpretation and representations of art inside and outside of school. An important reason for reassessing the ways in which we teach visual culture is that the boundaries between visual forms are breaking down, presenting new possibilities for interpretation as a foundation for learning and resulting in a new challenge in curriculum development. In this chapter, I give attention to the analysis of concepts that can provide a foundation for curriculum development.

Ways in which conceptions of curriculum in general education can inform art education are discussed in Chapter 6. Conceptions of curriculum structures and problems related to curriculum as a form of cultural representation are highlighted. The maintenance of democratic principles in education is discussed in ways that contrast with traditional arguments for an emphasis on the fine arts as the way to provide students with cultural capital. From a visual culture perspective, cultural capital is a much broader notion involving not only an awareness of high culture, but a social responsibility for visual culture at large.

Chapter 7 focuses on the visual technologies that have been mentioned throughout the book, and they are discussed in terms of teaching. Technology has made visual culture more readily accessible than literary forms of culture. The power of visual technologies from an educational perspective is profound and critically important to students' understanding of the pervasive visual arts.

Chapter 8 concludes the book, with a discussion of the importance of critical reflection during student production and critique as a democratic process. The discussion includes examples of the ways in which the visual arts will become an increasingly influential means of expression, communication, and identity construction.

Because this book is intended for students who have different levels of background knowledge in the field, as well as for professionals, I have tried to focus less on analyzing the work of individual theorists and more on the ways in which theories have been used. I hope that this ties the two sections of the book together and supports the idea that analysis should take place on multiple levels.

This book is an attempt to critique current assumptions about curriculum and reconnect wide-ranging visual arts forms and ideas that have been disconnected in curriculum. This disconnection is acted out at all levels of education and has been illustrated by the organization of the visual arts fields. The separations between primary, secondary, and higher art education and between the art education in schools and other cultural locations, such as in museums, in community programs, and on the web have long been problematic. Course boundaries based primarily on differences in media techniques now make less sense at a time when many professional artists regularly switch media, and the separation of fine arts from popular arts reduces opportunities for studying their connections. Advancing knowledge of visual culture depends on good foundations at all levels, including connections as well as distinctions between and among forms, ideas, and processes of visual culture.

TEACHING
VISUAL CULTURE

CHAPTER 1

The Professional Field

Theorizing Visual Culture in Education

IN POSTINDUSTRIAL, ADVANCED DEMOCRACIES THE VISUAL
arts are increasingly understood as infused into daily life through the
mass media, malls and amusement parks, local sculpture gardens, the
Internet, fashion and furniture design, and so on. What was once considered an elite and isolated form of human production is becoming
increasingly realized as a part of daily life. The visual arts are expanding not only in their forms, but in their influence through connections
to the range of social issues, including issues not always thought of as
social in character, such as ecology and conceptions of self. As a result,
the visual arts have become fundamental to the cultural transformation of political discourse, social interaction, and cultural identity that
characterizes the postmodern condition (Jameson, 1984, 1991). This
transformation is played out through broad cultural and interpersonal
interactions in social environments and institutions, including those
that are educational. Even environments not previously considered
educational have become so as a result of the didactic power of the visual arts. Their immediacy, memorability, and sensuality make the
visual arts particularly powerful as a symbolic form and this power
includes a didacticism that not only teaches us to want to decode their
messages, but can cause us to learn even when the message is unclear.

The visual arts make up most of visual culture, which is all that is
humanly formed and sensed through vision or visualization and shapes
the way we live our lives. Use of the term *visual culture* inherently
provides context for the visual arts in its effects and points to the connections between popular and fine arts forms. It includes the fine arts,
tribal arts, advertising, popular film and video, folk art, television and
other performance, housing and apparel design, computer game and
toy design, and other forms of visual production and communication.

1

Visual culture is inherently interdisciplinary and increasingly multi-modal. All of the arts, not just the arts traditionally considered visual arts, have visual culture characteristics. However, just as the definition of the term *art* has been debated for centuries, the term *visual culture* does not necessarily require a precisely agreed upon definition to discuss it in terms of education. Quite the contrary, it is likely that the multiple definitions of art that have been encouraged through formal and informal education have helped to keep art fresh and in the process of change.

An education in the visual arts takes place in and through the realm of visual culture, inside and outside of schools, at all educational levels, through the objects, ideas, beliefs, and practices that make up the totality of humanly conceived visual experience; it shapes our thinking about the world and leads us to create new knowledge through visual form. Art education, in its institutional and noninstitutional settings, whether conducted in a K–12 classroom or a university school of art, whether in a drawing lesson or as part of an interdisciplinary science unit, helps to develop rich meanings through life experience inside and outside of school. It is found in classrooms, museum galleries, community centers, people's homes, on the street, and in movie theaters. Informal art education happens throughout our lives as we encounter visual culture and have thoughtful discussions or debates about it.

At all levels, an education in visual culture in the 21st century must take into account this changing landscape of the visual arts and their didactic influence. Just as physics education is about the movements of bicycles as much as the movements of planets, art education is about the objects, meanings, purposes, and functions of the visual arts students make and see every day as much as the art in museums.

VISUAL CULTURE, EDUCATION, AND IDENTITY

An important educational aspect of visual culture is its effect on identity, in terms of both art-making and viewing, which is perhaps the greatest issue in education. Education is a process of identity formation because we change as we learn; our learning changes our subjective selves. The creation of self is based on the subject being invested with certain characteristics through symbolic representation (Lacan, 1977). The effects of images shape an individual's self-concept, even in the ways they shape the notion of individualism. Individuals appropriate characteristics of visual representations, adopting these representations as a description of himself/herself. From this perspective, people can be manipulated through images that are often antithetical to their individual natures (Baudrillard, 1983). However, the manipulation itself can seem to become a natural part of identity. Baudrillard, Harvey (1989), and other postmodern theorists point particularly to developments in technology, advanced levels of industrial capitalism, and totalizing mass media as initiating negative social conditions. However, Lyotard (1984) argues that a therapeutic value of art is found in contemporary imagery, as in advertising, that celebrates sensuality, promoting the natural flow of desire, and intensifying feeling.

The educational importance of visual culture is important to understand if we are to teach appropriately in a contemporary democracy. The new conditions of visual culture illustrate that personal freedoms no longer only involve matters of free speech. They concern freedom of information in a range of visual art forms integral to the creation of individual and group knowledge. People cannot only speak freely; they can visually access, display and duplicate, computer manipulate, and globally televise. Visual culture images and objects are continuously seen and instantaneously interpreted, forming new knowledge and new images of identity and environment. It mediates social relationships between and among makers and viewers and among viewers. Art and art education are forms of mediation between people in which a range of professional, discursive practice plays an important role.

Discursive Relations and Cultural Mediation

Theory in the human sciences is tied to historical shifts in discursive relations (Foucault, 1970). Theories change or remain stable in relation to social conditions, such as social values, national and international policies, and the advancement of technologies, as well as new factual information. For example, what has been thought proven is often later called into question because our vision of what is possible changes over time and representations of new possibilities emerge. Such changes in theory both shape and reflect shifts in professional discourse and discursive relations, such as power arrangements and social patterns. People can be included or excluded through discourse. They can gain power by adopting a discourse viewed as legitimate by people who have power.

Discursive relations have become increasingly visual and visual symbols are often used as a form of discourse. Discursive relations are established by a wide range of visual interactions; for example, through the professional work of artists and critics; as a result of advertising that sells us (advertisers say "educates" us about) things the advertisers claim we do not yet know we need; or by television "talk shows" that have provided a medium for at least one reported real-life murder when people made private life public. The discourse of cultural critique has become particularly powerful through the use of visual forms. From work of the artists who call themselves the Guerrilla Girls to film clips used on television news programs people respond to social conditions through visual culture.

Such discursive relations may seem hidden, or only implied, by the often distant interaction between makers and viewers, but the visual arts do mediate social interactions between people. Art is a form of social production and the creation of a work of art is only.part of the product; it is the viewer that completes the work and what is produced is a social relationship.

At least three types of human interaction with information exists in contemporary society: face-to-face, mediated, and mediated quasi-interaction (Thompson, 1994). Face-to-face interaction is a dialogic relationship between people in the same space and time. Mediated interaction is also dialogic, but is dependent on a form of mediation between people who are not in the same location, such as a personal letter or telephone call. Mediated quasi-interaction is monologic, involving a one-way transmission of information through space and time. People respond in many ways to image carriers, such as books, films, television, fine art, and the web, and this third type of interaction involves vast audiences and does not demand a reflective response.

Teaching visual culture mediates both at the level of its content (that is, the visual arts mediate between makers and viewers) and at the level of curriculum development and enactment. Curriculum can be understood as an interaction between students and a range of people through texts and images. Consider the case of published curriculums (national, textbook, and so on). A published curriculum is developed for a large audience. Its authors stake out the ground that a particular group has decided should be "covered" (Apple, 1986). The curriculum mediates interactions between the author of the text and the teacher who, with the students, performs the act of local appropriation. The published curriculum is monological; but the teaching and learning are dialogical. Cultural institutions, such as school and museums, are some of the few structured, dialogical environments that students have access to in which sense can be made of their many monological experiences.

Interpretive Communities

Images objectify meaning that is at once transitory and tightly bound to the object. The process of objectification emerges through interpretations of the relationship among what is represented, the object representing, and the representation. When we refer to art in education, the interpretation process is complex. Art (e.g., a painting) can be used to objectify objects (dishes and fruit arranged on a table), but education objectifies that which objectifies (the still life painting). This means that art educators must constantly be aware that they are representing a representation, interpreting an interpretation.

Although some educators argue that they "start" with the art object when teaching, interpretations discussed in class are part of a history of discourse from previous social settings developed by artists, teachers, students, curators, and so on. Without an understanding of the importance and influence of this wide-ranging discussion across time and space, students may get the impression that a single answer is correct, preferences are only personal, or that interpretation is solely dependent upon what is depicted in an image. A classroom in which visual culture is made and discussed is part of an interpretive learning community.

The interpretation of newly encountered images is based on meanings that have been defined through the previous use of related signs. This intergraphical process is didactic because it involves meanings that are learned and taught by social groups (Freedman, 1994). Images are related to previous knowledge, integrated with other images that have been created by other people, and recalled for various purposes, including the purpose of interpreting and creating new images. Through mixes of popular visual culture and fine art, new images are produced and new meanings of art (as a category) emerge. In the process, what it means to be "cultured" is transformed.

Although aesthetic knowledge has been represented at times as being frivolous or trivial, it is actually a critically important type of practical knowledge (Bourdieu, 1993). For example, the knowledge on which taste is based has long been considered a form of cultural capital and it is important to demonstrate that one has this knowledge in order to succeed in the context of an economy based on such capital. This is the case at all socioeconomic levels. The wealthy indicate wealth through "tasteful" practices, such as collecting fine art. People who do not collect fine art also demonstrate tastes that indicate group memberships and individual identities.

THEORIZING THE PROFESSIONAL FIELD

One important practical use of aesthetic knowledge is that of cultural critique. Cultural critique is a constructive force in arts communities precisely because it opens discussion that might otherwise be closed. Many types of critique related to art and education exist, ranging from critical social theory, to art criticism, to classroom critique. Critique helps participants not only make judgments and reflect on their own positions, but realize that the discourse of their positions, the critique, the curriculum, the field, and so on, create the milieu of possibility. With the increasing prevalence of the visual arts, critique in and about art education is an important democratic process.

Critical Social Theory Foundations

Two strains of critical theory from other countries have particularly influenced U.S. thinking about art and education since the 1960s. The first was European neo-Marxist theory, particularly the work of critical sociologists of the Frankfurt School, such as the aesthetics of Theodor Adorno. The second strain was Brazilian educator Paulo Freire's theory that grew out of efforts to promote literacy borrowed from John Dewey's pragmatism and ideas about progressive education. These social theories were vehicles for responding to political and economic oppression. In part, their translation in the United States was a response to the personal isolation of existentialism and the extreme individualism that developed after the Second World War, as a result of fears of authoritarianism and anticommunist sentiments. These theories were translated into general education in order to address the problem of an increased asocial, technization of curriculum, such as the development of "teacher proof" curriculum. The historicism of the Frankfurt School provided a way of escaping the ahistorical grip of logical positivism and reconnecting various modern practices to their traditions. In art theory, the conceptual shift from modernism to postmodernism supported artists as they revisited social content and revealed historical connections to their art and popular culture.

By the 1970s and 1980s, the U.S. version of neo-Marxist theory and Freire's "pedagogy of the oppressed" became entangled in education with feminist and cultural theory related to civil rights. Ideas were taken from each and adapted to fit into North American contexts. For example, U.S. poststructuralists and other postmodernists rejected Marxism as a meta-narrative and feminists and cultural theoreticians pointed out that neo-Marxist theory, although helpful in uncovering historical dimensions of oppression related to economics, did little to aid in the understanding of complex cultural, social, and personal issues.

At the same time, poststructuralists also questioned taken-for-granted educational structures, including the modernist, bureaucratic, and pseudoscientific foundations on which schooling is built (Cherryholmes, 1988). They pointed to the lived experience of teachers and students and to the contributions of ambiguity, conflict, and resistance to teaching and learning. When people used the term *critical theory* as applied to education, it had a range of meanings, from poststructuralists' challenge to the notion of a single, correct, or even best structure (for example, a best institutional organization, artistic interpretation, or lesson plan) to analyses of curriculum based on the socioeconomic conditions of certain populations. However, all referred to critical reflection at a social level.

In the 1980s critical social theory became part of the discourse of art education and fueled the growth of social perspectives of the field that lead to broader conceptions of teaching visual culture. In the United States, the fuel came in part from the work of art educators who had grown up in the 1960s and who as youngsters had taken part in civil rights marches and demonstrations against the Vietnam War. Their convictions about the relationship between aesthetic meanings and social justice were long held and strongly felt and are now being revealed in the struggle to change art education.

In the last chapter of this book, the concept of critique is both broadened and made specific on the level of analyzing student work. Critique is conceptualized as a form of social knowledge production done in the context of a cultural milieu of art program evaluation and student assessment.

Defining the Intellectual Field

Sociologist Pierre Bourdieu's work concerning symbolic practices can aid in the development of an understanding about the breadth of art education and its character as part of the social world. Bourdieu's attempt to found a science of aesthetic knowledge began with *The Love of Art*, first published in French in 1966. He has done substantial and creative analyses of artistic perception and appreciation, including studies of museum audiences, collecting, and artistic preferences. Bourdieu's work is rare in that he draws on empirical evidence in the development of a theory of art that is formed through the symbolic practices of a larger economy.

According to Bourdieu, certain practices in an intellectual field lead people to think and act in ways consistent with the education connected to the field. These ways of thinking and acting then become part of the social and historical structure that forms the medium for professional practice. Bourdieu (1993) argues that different intellectual fields have a different internal logic and their own peculiarities. An intellectual field is not an integrated whole, but rather involves an agreed-on set of contested sites (Foucault, 1966/1970) or conflicts that expand and contract as new debates and practices emerge and old ones are revisited. These reflect the internal logic of a field, as well as the habitus related to its cultural production (Bourdieu, 1993).

Bourdieu's work in areas concerning aesthetics falls short at times, in part as a result of his own professional field. As a sociologist, Bourdieu understands little of what it means to create a work of art and has excluded the whole creative process in his theory, which is surprising neglect considering his work on the notion of practice. Bourdieu establishes a continuum between high art and popular forms of art, which, although represented as being on opposite ends of the continuum, are inherently joined by it. For Bourdieu, the influence of individuals in art or education is of little importance and in the complex context of most postindustrial countries, Bourdieu's understanding of art is too linear (as is his conception of learning). However, his work is widely acknowledged as the most comprehensive attempt to theorize art, education, and other social fields in a sociological framework to date and as taking a major step toward a new understanding of aesthetics.

Bourdieu and other theorists have argued that education is reproductive—that is, it reproduces the culture in which it is carried out. Professional education makes this possible by teaching new members of the professional community to reproduce the field as they reproduce other cultural knowledge. However, education is not only reproductive; it is also productive. This is particularly true in the case of the arts where the value of originality is imparted at the same time as the value of following rules. If one thinks of art and education as completely separate intellectual fields, this would be a contradiction. However, as part of the intellectual field of art education, it is the perimeter of practice.

So, what is the intellectual field of art education? It is the realm of thought within which practice exists that concerns what, why, and how we come to know about visual culture. It is part of the larger fields of cultural production, economy, politics, and so on. It takes into account the range of visual images, objects, ideas, and practices that mediate between and across human beings and the environment. Students, teachers, artists, and curriculum theorists take part in the intellectual field, which is interpreted and reinterpreted. The intellectual field is enabled through the knowledgeable creation and viewing of visual culture. It is the intersection of the fields of art and education and it shapes how people, including artists, think about art. In a sense, art produces curriculum as curriculum produces art.

The ways in which people conceptualize their professional domain are important because they shape the theories that influence practice.

Although theories of art and education are usually thought of as intending to describe reality, they often function in ways that construct reality by categorizing, organizing, and providing a discourse for art education that can limit, as well as enable, possibilities. Theorizing at the juncture of art and education is dependent upon social issues, such as professional interests, disciplinary boundaries, and territories of value.

REMNANTS OF SOCIAL THEORY THAT SHAPE SOCIAL PRACTICE: LESSONS FROM THE HISTORY OF ART EDUCATION

The variety of forms and functions of visual culture that have long been included in education have typically been included as a form of art education. Consider public school curriculum. In the late 1800s, industrial drawing practices brought from England and Germany were the first required visual art education in the United States. In the early 1900s, students learned moral values and aesthetics from the study of pictures. In the 1920s, children's self-expression through art became an important part of a therapeutic post-World War education, and in the 1930s the aesthetics of everyday life gained popularity during the Great Depression. As a result of this history, art education is a good place to start an investigation of visual culture in educational contexts.

Stories of the past can help us understand that art education has continually changed in response to contemporary experience, while at the same time helping to maintain larger social structures of a culture and its institutions. The social structure has supported the reproductive aspects of educational practice, yet at the same time has been the medium within which new theories have developed about art and education. Theory and practice are creatively productive, as well as reproductive, and it is because of this interactive relationship that remnants of theory continue to exist in schools, museums, and other educational settings even as change takes place.

As a result, change in art education, like other social change, must be considered in relation to the larger historical picture. Even when the time seems short, the assumptions and activities that are part of change are conditions of time and place outside, as well as inside, the professional field. Structure maintains values and ideals, such as the ideal of individualism, in institutions and in consciousness. At the same time, such structure contains elements of transformation. For example, in a sociohistorical structure that maintains the whole societal ideal of individualism, individual and group differences will be apparent and initiate change. In advanced industrial countries, transformation emerges from such cultural contradictions tied to moral positions (Habermas, 1976).

The Structure of Modern History:
The Enlightenment as a Foundation for Art Education

An important historical consideration in understanding current practice in art education is the structure of the Enlightenment. The philosophical debate that emerged in Europe in the 17th and 18th centuries concerning the character of knowledge, nature, and culture enabled both progressive thought and its internal contradictions, and was instrumental in shaping change in art and education. It provided the medium for avant-garde art, a democratic society, the ideal of free information, a popular mass media, a commitment to individualism, and an industrial and postindustrial capitalist economy. It has also provided the possibility for professional elitism, partisan politics, mass distribution of violent pornography and propaganda, mass social control, alienation, and extreme poverty even in the wealthiest nation in the world.

From the enlightened 18th century perspective, knowledge existed in a natural form that had been hidden by the interests of a corrupt clergy and greedy aristocracy. The new intellectuals of the 18th century argued that these authorities had artificially constructed social conventions and imposed them on individuals in order to maintain their social positions. The French and American revolutions, and other responses to authoritarian regimes, confounded tradition by demonstrating that the politics and social arrangements of the day were not natural and necessary. The debate focused on the idea that men (specifically) had natural civil rights, including a right to knowledge and freedom from political oppression.

In contrast to a culture based on beliefs and interests, enlightened knowledge was considered rational and disinterested. Men were suddenly thought to be logical, to have free will, and to be in control of their own destiny. However, enlightened philosophy also impressed ideal, human qualities on nature (Eagleton, 1983). Culture was criticized as an imposition on free will; yet the emergence of enlightened science was created as a field of knowledge based on human values. Scientific knowledge was to be discovered and used for the collective human good. It was to direct, as well as to help, people to live naturally and humanely. The enlightened "man" was to act rationally and progressively to maintain individual freedom and control the forces of nature.

Modern Oppositions: The Example of Gender

The structure of the Enlightenment has been maintained and yet changed through its internal contradictions. These internal contradictions are exemplified by the conception of women's place in nature and culture (e.g., Jordanova, 1980; Schwartz, 1984). At one level, women were thought of as more "natural" and uncivilized than men. This was considered proven by women's ability and taken-for-granted desire to give birth and by women's presumed irrationality. On another level, women were presumed to be more social than men (who were considered naturally independent) and were to socialize men in order to form families. A woman was supposed to provide a family and home that was dependent on a man, but was also supposed to make him dependent on her in order to keep him in the family unit (Schwartz, 1984).

While individuals were conceptualized as agents of change, the idea of natural free will was internally conflicted because only certain types of people were considered to be individuals. The struggle to destroy authoritarian institutions contained the assumption that each person was to be a free actor, implying that individuals could act on all possibilities. However, being an individual meant something different for people of different races, classes, and sexes.

Structure has been maintained but ruptured by responses to these contradictions. For example, at one level, what it means to be a woman has been transformed by the requirements of thinking and acting consistently with male social systems in order to gain power. At another level, the systems themselves have been transformed through the crisis of women's transformation (Douglas, 1977).

Foundations of Modern Art and Postmodern Responses

These were ideals of modernism and were reflected in the modern art of the 19th and 20th century. For example, in Goya's *Third of May, 1808*, an early modern painting, the basic narrative is fairly clear to people familiar with the cultural context. Before discussing the painting with my students, I have asked them to tell the suggested story. They understand who the artist intends them to sympathize with because he has shown the individuality of the peasants about to be shot by the French soldiers. The soldiers, in contrast, are without faces; they have no identity except their guns and uniforms, which are symbols of oppression. The central heroic figure in the painting, shown in the purity of a white shirt, stands in a martyred position with his arms outstretched as the soldiers take aim to fire. Other peasants are at his feet in a dark landscape. The landscape is lit by a single lamp on the ground, creating the dramatic underlighting effect of a theatrical scene that captures a moment in time. Although complex in its narrative, this modern painting reflects rationalism and is painted in a single, meta-narrative style that is easily described at a surface level based on general, Euro-American (Christian) cultural knowledge, such as an understanding of oppositions like good versus evil and strong versus weak.

The ideals of the Enlightenment are still at the center of advanced democratic culture, which exemplifies the interactive relationship between modernism and postmodern life. However, international critiques of cultural conditions have revealed a profound disillusionment about the limitations of rationalism as conceived in the Enlightenment project (Bernstein, 1986). This disillusionment has grown as the internal contradictions of the structure of the enlightened vision have become increasingly realized and criticized. In part, the realization and critique has been theorized through analyses of the new "technologies" of psychological and social control (Foucault, 1970). Michel Foucault analyzed these technologies using the examples of sexuality and mental illness, and others have used his methods to analyze the ways in which schooling functions as a form of social control. The often subtle technologies of the mind—which include institutions other than schools, such as the mass media, and which have become increasingly visual—were developed, legitimated, and function on the basis of the rationality and discursive practices intended to support the ideals of enlightened humanism. And yet, at the same time, they control the lives of individuals and social groups, often contradicting the ideals of freedom reflected by the arts. There is concern that such technologies may be even more insidious than the physical controls they replaced because psychological control is viewed as scientific (and therefore natural and disinterested).

The postmodern condition is wrapped in these concerns. Postmodernism in art and general culture is a response to the realization of the Enlightenment—not in its ideal form, but in the form of a modernism that provided the possibility for physical and psychological technologies that have negative, as well as positive, outcomes. Acceptance of such lived complexities—and the denial of the simple dichotomies, monocultural universality, and "scientific" solutions of functional rationality—are part of the postmodern condition (Lyotard, 1984) and one of the reasons that art is considered a metaphor for postmodernism just as science is for modernism.

In contrast to the earlier discussion of Goya's painting, consider a postmodern work by Robert Longo entitled *Still* (1984). Longo's piece is made up of five large panels, each with a different, highly representational image. From left to right, the first panel is a picture of a hand holding a human heart, the second image is of a female nude seated on a bed looking away from the viewer, the third panel is a large black bird with spread wings, the fourth panel is solid black, and the fifth panel is a knight in armor on a horse. In contrast to the apparent single narrative of the Goya painting, this work seems to defy narrative; and yet it suggests many possible, even conflicting, stories (about love, sex, death, medicine, and so on), which shifts the focus from understanding the intent of the artist to an interactive relationship between artist, object, and viewer. Teaching about postmodern works of art cannot depend on oppositions, such as accurate versus inaccurate interpretation, or even original versus unoriginal. Rather than being oppositional, and resolving into one of opposed sides, the realm of understanding postmodern visual culture is multidimensional. Artists set up parameters within which viewers can move closer to the artists' intentions as they gain more knowledge about their work. However, the purpose of study is to develop deeper, richer, and more complex knowledge, which often causes conflicts of opinion rather than resolutions.

The postmodern condition is where we find ourselves as we wrestle with the inequities and contradictions of an enlightened vision that is a foundation of public schooling. Although many of the foundational ideals of the Enlightenment are still valued—and from an artistic and educational perspective, critically important—its enactment to maintain those ideals is a struggle that must be continually reflected upon and critiqued. In a sense, postmodern theory seeks to reveal what is hidden in modernism; it is to challenge underlying assumptions and that which has been taken for granted. As a result, we can more clearly see the contradictions of functional rationality in the professional field, such as the immense commerce surrounding the production of visual culture, which depends so much on learning about and appreciating art, and yet results in so little money being given to art in education. An example of functional rationality in curriculum is the use of scientific rhetoric to frame curriculum and the professional field.

BREAKING BOUNDARIES AND TEACHING CONCEPTS

Representations are pastiches (Barthes, 1974) or cultural collages (Clifford, 1988). They are made up of and refer to a combination of possible meanings, rather than a single, unified, intended meaning. A realm of meanings is interpreted and loosely attached to signs that people construct and informally teach each other in order to facilitate communication. This is the reason that we can revisit rich examples of visual culture and continue to develop new meanings through our new experiences with them, regardless of whether we are in a museum looking at a Renaissance painting or *Star Wars* fans seeing one of the films for the 10th time.

The ways we represent through the realm of visual culture shapes people's thinking. From an educational standpoint, understanding the importance of representation is critical because we can help direct the construction of knowledge in ways that enrich students' experiences with art. However, we can also direct it in ways that limit that enrichment. For example, if we represent art knowledge in education as being conceptually located within each of a few discrete fine art disciplines, we are suggesting a very different way of thinking about the visual arts than if we represent art as being inherently interdisciplinary and widely suggestive. Many forms of visual culture cross over boundaries even within the form. As illustrated in Figure 1.1, the architecture of a shopping mall could be seen as crossing the boundaries between fine art and popular culture.

Figure 1.1. Photograph illustrating shopping mall design.

Photo: Kerry Freedman

In the postmodern world, *what* students come to know and *how* they come to know breaks traditional boundaries. Currently, students may gain more information from images than from texts. As a result, art education is an increasingly important responsibility as the boundaries between education, high culture, and entertainment blur and students increasingly learn from the visual arts. In the context of changing visual culture, an investigation of challenges to the boundaries of form, the boundaries of the object, and the boundaries of school subjects is in order.

Another important aspect of border crossing has to do with cultural and educational borders. Teaching visual culture includes many visual cultures. It is fundamentally about the inclusion of people and the images and artifacts they conceive and create. Inclusion of visual culture of the past is part of this consideration of diverse cultures and subcultures.

The border crossing also involves a questioning of the traditional separation between producer and spectator and the separation of education levels. As will be discussed in Chapter 4, audiences are now thought of as having an important role to play in the construction of meaning involving visual culture, and educational audiences must rehearse throughout their schooling related concepts and skills in order to build knowledge. Art education at all levels is becoming increasingly important, as is making complex curriculum connections among different levels of education. In the past, much of what was expected from the elementary and secondary levels was an education in formal and technical qualities to develop those skills in the students who would go on to become art majors in higher education. An education that interrelates visual culture experiences across elementary, secondary, and higher education levels responds to the fact that visual culture has become increasingly more accessible, interactive, and dependent upon broad audience viewing habits. For example, many adolescents watch the same television programs that adults find entertaining, younger and older children play the same computer games, and children visit museums with their parents. University schools of art now include courses on computer graphics animation in which students learn to make those television programs, computer games, and films.

Challenging the Boundaries of Forms

The visual arts now overlap so much of social life that curriculum must be considered within the larger realm of visual culture, if for no other reason than to contextualize and help make sense of the visual arts. But other reasons exist, the first of which is that the boundaries of visual form types have collapsed. Artists less often specialize in painting on canvas or sculpting in marble. Artists cross boundaries, such as the Catalan artist Antoni Tàpies who "paints" with ground marble. "His paintings' surfaces often resemble walls and their abundant inscriptions (of signs, letters, and words) associate them with graffiti" (Encounters, 2000, p. 275). The artist has stated that his "works are often paintings, objects, and poetry in one" (Encounters, 2000, p. 275). Painters do performance art, performers do rock videos, video artists recycle film clips, filmmakers use computer graphics which are then adapted for advertising, and advertisers appropriate paintings.

Visual culture often involves contested boundaries between traditional and new visual forms. As well as including painting and sculpture, computer graphics, fashion design, architecture, television, comics and cartoons, magazine advertisements, and so on, visual culture overlaps with arts not usually categorized as visual, such as dance, theater, television, and film. Sophisticated and educational semiotic analyses can as easily be done of a Grateful Dead event as of a work of fine art (Smith-Shank, 1996). The visual arts are seen at NASA and Disneyland, as well as at the Louvre, and are connected to various other art forms. Through visual connections, these arts become part of visual culture, just as music is connected to visual culture through, for instance, rock videos. As art critics in the mid-20th century understood, words are an important additional modality for learning about painting, just as listening to music is for dance and dance is for music.

A critical debate in the arts and education concerns the place of visual forms produced through the use of computer and other advanced technologies. The debate is also about the dissemination of visual culture, including traditional arts forms, through the use of these technologies. Computer technology is not only a medium—it is a means—and it is largely experienced as visual. It has enabled people to see things previously unimagined, to cross borders of traditional form in the fine arts, to the mass media, and to scientific visualization.

In the face of these contemporary conditions, it seems less important than it once was to focus education on making distinctions of taste or between "higher" and "lower" arts as ways of defining the content domain of the field. Such distinctions continue to be important to understanding aspects of artistic practice, such as the enactment of different artistic intentions, private collecting, professional training, museum exhibition, and the use of fine art in advertising. And, in fact, differentiating forms simplifies the visual arts and helps to make them administratively and conceptually manageable. However, we now live in a complex era and even highly specialized professionals realize that solving some of the most serious and important problems of the world demands interdisciplinary and cross-disciplinary knowledge.

Challenging the Boundaries of Objects

A second reason for considering the focus of curriculum as including the larger realm of visual culture is the changing character of art objects. Historically, visual arts curriculum has been based more on the concept of the fine art object exemplar (their production, history, criticism, and aesthetic), rather than on the range of other artifacts. This is an "academic" approach to curriculum, as opposed to a humanist or social reconstruction approach (McNeil, 1975, 1996). The purpose of the academic approach to curriculum is the dissemination of information from the professional disciplines and the conservation and maintenance of traditional knowledge. A strong emphasis on truth, and the search for it, is inherent to this approach. Important roots of this approach date from the 18th century; however, a resurgence of the approach followed the Second World War when international competition became an increasingly important political and economic issue.

Support for the academic approach to curriculum has come from a variety of sources, including contemporary scholars who subscribe to the idea that discretely different forms of knowledge exist. Howard Gardner (1991) supports this approach through his argument that students should be guided away from their intuitive understanding of the world toward knowledge developed by professional communities. The perspective of cultural literacy espoused by E. D. Hirsch and Allan Bloom supports this approach through its focus on schooling as a means of passing on traditions of "excellence."

However, the traditional academic approach raises several problems. First, regarding fine art, this approach has been adapted to K-12 curriculum based on narrow and prescribed behavioral learning objectives. Narrow learning objectives and assessment can result in curriculum that is about what can easily be taught and assessed, rather than what students should learn. The curriculum stays confined within the arena of fine art and the arena is defined mainly by its objects. From this perspective, other aspects of the fine arts, such as issues of gender, race, and socioeconomic conditions, are given little attention and treated as an "optional extra"—even when such issues are the point of the work.

Second, artistic objects are transformed through education and often lose their cultural identity. As the curriculum becomes more focused on objectives easily taught and assessed, exemplars (readily available through publications) are used over and over by instructors. Student teachers then use the same exemplars in their own teaching and, in the process, the artifacts become simplified and segmented. One painting is used to illustrate asymmetrical balance, another to exemplify the creation of texture through the use of a palette knife; their purpose is simplified and reified from the multiple and complex ideas on which the paintings were probably based to formal and technical qualities.

Third, the focus on fine art exemplars tends to imply a single line of Western stylistic development. Formal and technical qualities are considered to be the most important connecting concepts between art objects. Even the educational emphasis of content such as the figure, landscape, or still life, is taught as formal and technical. The interpretations and connections between these and other artifacts—the ideas between the art objects, which are often their reasons for being—are often missed. This is commonplace when students are told that they will be making an Impressionist painting with markers on construction paper. I have seen this lesson taught many times, even going so far as having all the students in the class draw the same vase and sunflowers. In fact, the students may be borrowing the technique of visual color mixing from the Impressionists, but they are certainly not making an Impressionist painting (and, why should they?).

Fourth, visual artists, including fine artists, have broken through the borders of "the object" in many ways and refocused attention on relationships between objects. As the boundaries of visual cultural forms have become blurred, objects have become recycled bits of other objects that are collaged together, copied, duplicated, and multiplied.

Challenging the Boundaries of School Subjects

A third reason that a focus of curriculum must be the larger realm of visual culture is that the objects of study defeat traditional art categories, as do the academic disciplines through which they are studied. Of course, categories and concepts are crucial for learning. We learn concepts by discriminating one thing from another. Before entering school, most children have learned to distinguish an animal from an automobile and a banana from a bunny. Making these distinctions helps children come to know the significant qualities of each. Whenever we learn a new concept, at whatever age, our preliminary processes of learning involve determining in what ways the concept is like and unlike concepts we already know. We attach new information to old knowledge, compare and contrast, and come to an understanding that will be continually adapted as we learn more. If learning is successful, the complexity of concepts becomes increasingly apparent, categories blur, and hard and fast distinctions become less discrete. However, in art curriculum, many of these boundaries have become reified. In some educational settings, art curriculum is the sum total of courses based on media skills, entitled for example, Beginning or Advanced Drawing, Painting I or II, or 2-D or 3-D Design. Not only is this type of curriculum unsuitable in the context of the work practices of contemporary artists who regularly cross over boundaries of media and technique; it misrepresents the realm of knowledge in and through the visual arts as being primarily technical.

Challenging the old constructs of knowledge about the visual arts leads to at least some degree of interdisciplinarity. The realm of the visual arts overlaps with other school subjects. Artists draw on all types of knowledge and cognitive processes to create. Therefore, it is less important to think of boundaries in this context than to find ways of addressing the range of content that will help students to understand the visual arts. Sharing content typically considered part of the domain of other school subjects can only help students to understand the importance and power of the visual arts and their place in the world. Art education should help students know the visual arts in their complexity, their relationships as well as their independences, their conflicting ideas as well as their accepted objects, and their connections to social thought as well as their connections to other professional practices.

CONCLUSION

Many years ago, as an undergraduate, I was taught, in no uncertain terms, that fine art was different from other forms of visual art by virtue of its creators' intentions to produce objects primarily for the purpose of aesthetic appreciation. I spent much of my higher education studying cogent arguments as to the higher purposes of the fine arts and their greater conceptual complexity in contrast to more popular visual forms. Whether supported by Bell's formalism, Janson's art history, or Croce's expressivism, education was consistent on a critical issue: fine art was a distinct category and the sole art category that should receive attention in education. Though following on the heels of the critique of this distinction even by fine artists themselves, the view that the distinction should exist remained strong in education.

This view may have been easy to hold before the use of computers and other advanced technologies changed the ways people made and saw the visual arts. The belief system on which this view is based was established before a film set design could be created in its entirety inside a computing machine, before the first music video was shown on MTV, before a manipulated photograph could be sent all over the world in an instant, and before the exhibition of *Star Wars* costumes, set designs, and storyboards was shown in major art museums. This view was consistent with the idea that while fine art was truth and made life particularly acute, popular culture took students away from real life and dulled their senses and imaginations.

However, things have changed. Fine art is still critically important, but it is only one form of visual culture worthy of study. Visual culture as a whole must be seen as real in the sense that it is a major part of everyday experience. Fine art promotes and is promoted by the popular and can both excite students' imaginations and inform their creations. The argument for fine art as opposed to popular art forms based on conceptual complexity falls short when it is understood that fine art has become popular, as illustrated by the success of museums as tourist attractions, and the conceptual complexity of minimalist painting (even interpreted spiritually) pales next to *Star Trek—TNG. The Simpsons* is both popular and sophisticated because creator Matt Groening is an insightful artist. Visual culture is part of students' daily lives and they approach life based, in part, on their daily encounters with its diversity and complexity.

We are on the edge of a new artistic renaissance. Images are becoming more pervasive than texts, the visual arts are being seen by new audiences in new ways, and artistic methods, such as portfolio assessment, have gained currency even in general education. An essential responsibility of education in the future will be to teach students about the power of imagery and the freedoms and responsibilities that come with that power. If we want students to understand the postmodern world in which they live, curriculum will have to include a greater focus on the impact of *visual* forms of expression across traditional boundaries of teaching and learning, including boundaries of cultures, disciplines, and artistic forms.

The following concepts, which reflect this border crossing, are foundations of teaching visual culture:

1. *Reconceptualizing the field.* In the past, art education has focused to a great extent on objects of art, often fine art, per se. Now, greater attention is being placed on the importance of relationships between makers and viewers that develop through the mediation of objects.

These relationships are important as an educational topic because separating art from its intents and purposes, its interpretations and influences, and the power of its many forms, has led to a lack of understanding about the centrality of art to human existence.

2. *Meaningful aesthetics*. The range of visual forms can only be understood in relation to their contexts of making and viewing. At the same time, these contexts are shaped by visual culture forms. Curriculum is becoming more reflective of the contexts of the visual arts, thus including relevant information needed in order to understand the complexity of visual culture.

3. *Social perspectives*. The social life of visual culture is being redefined on a global scale as hybrid cultures are established and visual technologies shape the freedom of information crossing international borders. In postindustrial democracies, visual forms of expression and critique influence, as well as reflect, social life. The educative power of positions and opinions expressed by individuals and social groups through visual forms is a new emphasis in curriculum.

4 *Interactive cognition*. The importance of relationships between people and objects to learning is becoming more apparent as a result of new cognitive research. Differences in individual constructions of knowledge must now be taken into account, but at the same time, group cognition and situated cognition studies tell us that people come to know in relation to human and environmental contexts. Students create and interpret based on previous representations of knowledge, recycling the imagery and ideas they encounter. They come to know, in part, through interdisciplinary inquiry and developmental strategies, and should not be taught only based on the structure of professional disciplines.

5. *Cultural response*. Curriculum is increasingly including the visual arts of diverse cultural groups. Cultural difference is profoundly illustrated and supported through the visual arts. Multicultural, cross-cultural, and intercultural issues concerning the visual character of our social lives and environments are often the critical issues in art and the most important aspects of art to teach. Creation and interpretation are cultural as well as individual responses.

6. *Interdisciplinary interpretation*. Art education is now about visual culture, which includes *all* of the visual arts, including fine art, com-

puter games, manga, feature films, toy design, advertising, television programming, dreamtime paintings, fashion design, and so on. With the increasing and broadening influence of visual culture in society, the job of art educators has become vital to students' lives. As well as being the domain of art education, the immense scope and impact of visual culture should increase in significance across the curriculum.

7. *Technological experience.* Unlike drawing and painting, computer graphics allow people to create, copy, project, manipulate, delete, and reproduce images with an ease and speed that challenges traditional conceptions of talent and technique. In the process of reconfiguring the visual arts, advanced technologies have changed what it means to be educated.

8. *Constructive critique.* Knowledge is derived from a variety of sources outside of school, including visual culture. These fragmented, often contradicting, multidisciplinary, and intercultural references may have more to do with student understanding of a school subject than does curriculum based on the structure of a discipline. As a result, curriculum is beginning to include a greater focus on critical analyses of visual culture and on student assessment appropriate to the visual arts.

CHAPTER 2

Finding Meaning in Aesthetics

The Interdependence of Form, Feeling, and Knowing

EDUCATION IN AND THROUGH THE VISUAL ARTS IS NEEDED to support, and sometimes challenge, the increasingly sophisticated visual culture that has developed in postindustrial environments. In these environments, education can provide a way of enriching students' lives by helping them to critique and advance the ideas connected to visual culture and its meanings. The results of the *NAEP 1997 Arts Report Card: Eighth Grade Findings From the National Assessment of Educational Progress* (Persky, Sandene, & Askew, 1998) in the visual arts indicates that education has not been instrumental enough in promoting learning that will help students make meaning. In this study, students tended to have a basic knowledge of form and media, but found processes of connecting meaning to form particularly challenging. The results of this study raise the issue of the ways in which aesthetics are included in curriculum.

Definitions of aesthetic response, the conditions of aesthetic experience, descriptions of aesthetics objects, and aesthetic theorizing are at the foundation of curriculum, regardless of whether they are overtly addressed. Aesthetic judgments and particular models of aesthetics are explicitly stated or suggested in course texts and by individual teachers, even in the selection of visual culture to be shown in class.

Since the 1960s, attention has been increasingly given to making aesthetics overt in K–12 art curriculum by, for example, teaching the elements and principles of art and design as aesthetic qualities, addressing the "big" questions of art and aesthetics, and discussing the work of aestheticians as a professional field. The promotion of discipline-based art education by the J. Paul Getty Foundation in the 1980s and

1990s stimulated an even greater focus on the topic, resulting in research on learning about aesthetics, published recommendations by scholars on the teaching of aesthetics, and debates in the field of art education as to when and which aesthetic concepts should be introduced to children.

This increased attention to aesthetics as an overt part of curriculum demands an analysis of the particular conceptions of aesthetics focused upon in education and is specifically related to teaching visual culture. Such an analysis includes a consideration of the conditions of aesthetic experience in contemporary life and recent philosophical writing about visual culture.

THE MULTIPLE LEVELS OF AESTHETIC EXPERIENCE

Aesthetics is a two-sided coin. It is the beautiful, appealing, and intriguing that makes us want to look at visual culture. Aesthetics can promote feelings of righteousness, communicate vital messages, and illustrate excellence. These are the characteristics of visual culture that make us aware of the wonder of our perceptual systems and their complexities. And yet, they also remind us of our weaknesses. The same aesthetics that can uplift can lead us to believe what we see. Aesthetics can seduce us into adopting stereotypes, convince us to accept unrealistic body images, and persuade us to buy products without critical reflection.

As well as the dualistic quality of its impact, aesthetic response has multiple levels. To some extent, these levels of experience have been separated out and become bases for different, but related disciplines, such as analytic aesthetics, sociology of art, and semiotics. The connections between these disciplines have become more acute through the complex dynamics of postmodern image making and viewing that point to interdependent layers of daily and lifelong experience tied to aesthetic response. New forms of visual culture have been created, embodying a sophisticated aesthetic previously only imagined that make apparent levels of experience not previously considered. These changes force us to reconceptualize aesthetics as well as other philosophical concepts, such as knowledge, value, and identity.

Critical theorist Walter Benjamin argued that the industrialized world caused an atrophying of experience; it focused on the containment of shock, on predictability. This has certainly been a mission of public art education at all levels. However, surprise should be valued, particularly in the arts. As educators, we should continually hope for surprising crossings of aesthetic levels in the creation of knowledge, and for the unexpected outcome that surpasses planned objectives.

The range of aesthetic influences suggests that several aesthetic theories should be considered when teaching visual culture and that a contemporary education in aesthetics must respond to experiences inside and outside of school. In response, this chapter focuses on postmodern critiques of the analytic aesthetic tradition that has stood as the primary basis for theorizing art in education. In the first section of the chapter, a critique of the historical foundations of analytic aesthetics is presented. In the second section, historical and contemporary issues and problems related to the emphasis on formalism in curriculum are discussed. The third section focuses on the relationship of aesthetics to meaning in contemporary visual culture. In the final section of the chapter, John Dewey's ideas are revisited and a neopragmatist perspective of aesthetics is discussed.

FOUNDATIONS OF MODERNIST AESTHETICS

An important foundation of modernist aesthetics is the separation of theoretical knowledge, practical reason, and aesthetic judgment in Kant's *Three Critiques*, published in the late 18th century. Although aesthetic judgment was directly dealt with only in the third *Critique*, Kant's division of reason into different spheres set up an important problem for aesthetics. This separation helped to establish the idea that aesthetic judgments were made outside of cognition. Modern aesthetic theory (that is, aesthetic theory developed as part of the Enlightenment philosophical project) was founded on the Cartesian opposition of mind and matter and the ancient conflict between body and soul. The long-held belief that pure knowledge is objectified influenced Kant's interpretation of the ideal aesthetic experience as being self-contained and influenced interpreters of Kant who argued for the existence of an inherent aesthetic quality of fine art.

Postmodern philosophers convincingly argue that modernism prohibits self-criticism by limiting the boundaries of discussion; claiming rationality, objectivity, and authority; promoting universalism; and assuming progress. From this perspective, modernism is a curtain that postmodernism seeks to raise in order to reveal the contradictions, ambiguity, and irrationality of contemporary life. As philosopher Zygmunt Bauman (1993) states,

Modernity had the uncanny capacity for thwarting self-examination; it wrapped the mechanisms of self-reproduction with a veil of illusions without which those mechanisms, being what they were, could not function properly; modernity had to set itself targets which could not be reached, in order to reach what it could. The "postmodern perspective" ... means above all tearing off the mask of illusions. (p. 3)

In Kant's view, aesthetic judgment is grounded in a necessarily universal, immediate response of pleasure to certain objects perceived by the senses without concepts and involving no practical interests or desires. Kant conceived of a disinterested aesthetic experience of elation denying simultaneous (personal, social, economic, etc.) interests and elevating people to a higher plane of consciousness than that of everyday experience. Aesthetician Hilde Hein (1993) has argued that knowledge based on this view became an appropriation or objectification of experience, which opened up the possibility for a unique place of art, but closed off discussions of the breadth of art as it is actually experienced.

This aggressive act [of knowing] is performed by an agent, or subject, upon a passive object or subject-objectified. In knowing it, the subject exercises power over the object, demonstrating the capacity to control and bend it to the knower's will. Intellect masters nature, binding her to him in what Francis Bacon called a "chaste and lawful marriage." The highest form of knowledge is that in which the knower remains unmoved, aloof, and untouched by the object ... (p. 10)

From a historical perspective, it is understandable that the men who inscribed aesthetic theory sought an enlightened experience with beauty that was at once to possess and overcome the desire for possession. However, this personal and social struggle about desire, objectification, and possession became a universal theory of the aesthetic that defined both the appraisal of objects and the distinctions between them. Whether any experience is possible that isolates one from one's own interests is highly debatable, but nonetheless, this level of experience is a mere sensory coupling with a work of art, about which the viewer may know nothing. It is only the first, simple step toward developing an understanding of art and the much richer aesthetic experience that comes with depth of knowledge.

Although postmodern conditions accentuate connections between the levels of aesthetic experience, modernist, analytic aesthetics continues to underpin much curriculum practice. Analytic aesthetics is a perspective on theory about aesthetic experience and conditions that depends on breaking down experience into concepts and then constructing (or reconstructing) meaning based on the analysis. As will be discussed in the following sections, the roots of analytic philosophy emerged during the Enlightenment (and particularly from Kant's work) at a time important in the development of scientific method, but became particularly popular in 20th century Britain and North America.

MODERNIST AESTHETICS IN CURRICULUM

The emergence of modernity in art was closely tied to industrialization, the advancement of technology, and the movement of science toward increasing control and essentialism. The growth of aesthetic formalism, including its establishment in education, illustrates some of the ways in which visual experience is constructed within social systems. Formalism is a pseudoscientific conception of aesthetics developed in the late 19th and early 20th centuries at a time when science was gaining currency as applied to all areas of life. It focuses on the analysis of physical and perceptual characteristics of art objects and involves the reduction of form to elements (such as line, shape, and color) and principles (such as rhythm, balance, and unity) of design.

While this model of aesthetics appears only to facilitate an analysis of what is contained within a work of art, it has actually conditioned students to approach visual culture as a series of objects isolated from larger social meanings. Formalism has been so influential in the United States that it has become the definition of aesthetics in some American curriculum. In part, this is the case because the atomism and predictability of formalism is easily placed in curriculum and easily assessed. It can include the breaking down of visual form into component parts that neatly fit into the structure of curriculum as content is broken up into courses and lessons. This model of aesthetics does not include an analysis of use, function, underlying assumptions, social impact, and so on, because its application does not tend to take into account sociocultural aspects of visual culture. Nor does it promote an analysis of the creation of the model itself because it is presented as universal and timeless.

The assumption that any object can be effectively analyzed using such models carries with it the idea that the artifacts of any culture can appropriately be taught as if they were outside the context of time and place. This form of acculturation neither promotes an understanding of the peculiarities of fine art and aesthetics nor maintains the integrity of other forms of visual culture and alternative ways of understanding. In the past, the development of a disinterested appreciation of art required a good (Western) education and a relatively high socioeconomic level (Shusterman, 1992). However, the appreciation developed through education was tied to a variety of interests and desires; it not only gave authority to those who had such objects of achievement and abilities of appreciation, but caused people to want these objects and to work for them. Now, viewing is particularly complex because desire promoted by visual culture has overcome achievement (as illustrated by the hero effects of people in contemporary culture who are mere "media personalities").

The development of formalism by British aestheticians Roger Fry and Clive Bell around the turn of the 20th century was one response from the professional fine art community to abstraction and intercontinental influences from, for example, Africa and Asia. However, before discussing Fry and Bell, a look at the milieu of that time and place is necessary. In the late 19th century, British aesthetics included discussions of the importance of symbolic form.

The Rejection of Symbolism and the Emergence of Formalism

The symbolist community in Britain in the late 19th century focused on generating meaning through emotion as part of their rejection of naturalism. Delacroix and Baudelaire jointly promoted symbolism in their theorizing and their artistic production (one in painting, the other in poetry) through the use of metaphor and abstraction. In painting, the symbolists ranged from romantic symbolist artists to postimpressionists. The romantic symbolist painters, such as Dante Gabrielle Rossetti, Edward Burne-Jones, Gustave Moreau, and Odilon Redon, created stirring works symbolizing emotional states and sought to evoke these states in observers. They had a cross-disciplinary perspective of the arts and used terms such as "literary" and "musicality" to describe the relationships between symbols across art forms.

The postimpressionist symbolists—such as Paul Gauguin, Vincent Van Gogh, and Edward Munch—worked against the scientific aesthetic that was emerging at the time in favor of an aesthetic created through meaning. In part, their symbolist aesthetic resonates now because it illustrates the importance of social mediation between the internal, subjective and the external, objective realms. Their work is not only valued because of their topics, but also because the meaning of their art has grown over time as the lives of the artists, their social milieu, the contributions of their work to other artists, and so on, have added relevance to their work. However, interestingly, Gauguin and Van Gogh are most often included in K–12 curriculum for the formal qualities of their artistic styles.

James Whistler played an important role in the rejection of symbolism. He argued that art should exist for its own sake, rather than for conveying literary or moral ideas. Whistler's "The Ten O'Clock Lecture" (presented in 1885) was one of the early rejections of literary reference as a way of establishing value in the visual arts. Although he was a friend of symbolist artists and critics, such as Rossetti, he became a proponent of "pure form" that was investigated through his portraits and landscapes. Whistler sought to establish connections between the visual arts and music, often entitling his paintings in musical terms to draw attention to the importance and character of form. Interestingly, his best known painting, *Arrangement in Grey and Black: Portrait of the Painter's Mother*, is so powerfully symbolic that its mood and subject matter overtake attempts to focus solely on its formal qualities.

By the turn of the 20th century, British art critics Roger Fry and Clive Bell had conceptualized what would become universal, formalist arguments to explain impressionism and postimpressionism (but even Fry was concerned that his protégé Bell had gone too far). Fry had been asked to write a treatise supporting a universal theory of art that encompassed the so-called primitive art that was being newly appreciated by artists and collectors. Due to Fry's time commitments, Bell wrote the book. Bell's argument was that judgments of art must be made based on the significance of form regardless of content; that is, on the power of form to express ideals. This idea was also emerging in education as American art educator Arthur Wesley Dow worked to develop a system for teaching about art that crossed cultures. He had already begun developing models for art curriculum based on elements and principles of design that could explain the attraction of both Euro-American and Japanese composition.

The critical translation of Bell's work was established not through Bell's obtuse book itself, but through the simplifying mechanisms of early 20th-century curriculum. Generations of students have been taught to interpret Bell's writing as pertaining to form *without* content, thus ignoring a critical part of what is "significant" about form. To argue that the motivation behind Bell's work was unsound would be inappropriate. Formal characteristics cross various forms of visual culture, and in the time and place Bell wrote, his theory broadened the possibilities of art, promoting a type of valuing of diversity in the visual arts. However, it helped to establish an artificial dichotomy between form and content—not only content within a work of art per se, but extensions of interpretation outside the work. The problem was exacerbated in the application of the theory in curriculum as a separation of form from content and as the only, or first, way to analyze imagery. Perhaps it is only now that a rereading of Bell can be done in light of postmodern visual culture and a greater general awareness of the social influences of form.

The application of formalism in curriculum presented a dualistic problem. At one level, formalism enabled nonobjective art, "primitive" art, and children's art to be seen as art. But at another level, it closed off symbolic interpretation as a critical foundation of art education. It became the definition of aesthetics in education and in the process reduced the importance of social and cultural meanings of art in education.

Formalism and Expressionism in Mid-20th-century Art Criticism

In the United States, further distinctions between fine arts and popular arts resulted from a contemporary condition of industrialism, the emergence of the advertising industry (Bogart, 1995). Although fine artists and advertisers worked together in the early part of the century, by the 1920s, "self-proclaimed painters framed their identities, activities, goals, and the perceptions of their audience in terms of the expectations, practices, and publics defined by commercial discourses" (p. 206). American artists began to create an avant-garde milieu that rejected influence from outside individuals as a matter of formal purity, which we later see in the art criticism of Clement Greenberg and as a matter of self-expression in the work of Harold Rosenberg.

Greenberg and Rosenberg wrote art criticism advocating abstract expressionism as the first avant-garde art produced in the United States. Greenberg particularly sought distinctions between fine art and kitsch, which he criticized as representing the lower tastes of the masses. His perspective of fine art was based on positivism, the theory that all knowledge is derived from natural phenomena that can be studied and verified through the methods of empirical science. Greenberg's view of painting was evolutionary, reflecting the idea that the history of art was a developmental history of progress toward some end. The end Greenberg had in mind was to move ever closer to the surface (the formal and technical aspects of paint on canvas) and further away from illusions of representation and social meaning.

In contrast, Rosenberg was particularly interested in the expressive possibilities of action painting and the formal qualities of expression. He formed his view of art influenced by existentialism, a philosophy of confirming experiences of personal existence through radical freedom and responsibility. In his writing, he combined formalism and expres-

sionism; but unlike the German expressionists, who used style for social commentary, Rosenberg represented expression as originating inside the individual.

At one level, expressionism appears to involve a rejection of the
pseudoscientific character of formalism and to be more concerned with
generating meaning. However, abstract expressionism emerged in a
milieu of growing belief in the power of only certain psychological explanations of artistic creation and a therapeutic argument for the production of art based on emotional states as if these were distinct from
cognition and social life. Both Rosenberg and Greenberg were influenced
by their social environment. Like many members of the art community in the 1930s, Greenberg had been a member of the Communist
Party until the Soviet invasion of Poland. Greenberg's and Rosenberg's
ideas were shaped in part by the vast social and political ramifications
of World War II and influenced by the existential individualism that
followed. During the McCarthy era, when people in U.S. arts communities were being blacklisted for charges of communist affiliations,
Greenberg testified to a Senate subcommittee that modern art was politically neutral and had no social content. Of course, his denial was
political, as was the "neutral" art he defended.

In the context of this history, the development of formalism and
expressionism as a foundation for modernist curriculum makes sense.
Many of the people writing art curriculum today were educated as abstract expressionists and had a thorough grounding in Greenberg's and
Rosenberg's ideas about aesthetics. Although art education had been
in the public schools for more than a century, this was the period that
art curriculum became an issue to be studied, which may be one reason that aesthetics in curriculum continues to be tied to a translation
of the aesthetics of the period. In the 1960s and 1970s theoreticians in
art, such as John Berger and Marshall McLuhan, and in art education,
such as June King McFee and Vincent Lanier, argued for a broader approach to understanding visual culture. However, as will be discussed
in the next section, new conceptions of aesthetics (which reference the
past) have only now become an emphasis in education.

MEANING AND VISUAL CULTURE: MAKING
CONNECTIONS THROUGH ASSOCIATED KNOWLEDGE

The modernistic notion of aesthetic experience was a closed concept,
based on a limited general human experience with imagery, conceptu-

alized as disinterested and sublime, and shaped by the assumed existence of an inherent aesthetic quality. And yet, contemporary experience with the sophisticated visual culture we see every day, and the
knowledge we construct through our many overlapping and associative
visual experiences, tells us that the aesthetic exists in many forms and
is as interested as it is sublime. In order to illustrate this, we must re-
consider the place of formalism, distinctions between "high" and "low"
art, and social and other extended meanings. I address these in the following two sections.

The Interdisciplinary Character of Imagination

Visual culture is inherently interdisciplinary and many aspects of it
should be taught by crossing histories of cultures and technologies. For
most students not training to be arts professionals, it is probably less
important to understand art facts than it is for them to understand why
the arts exist, the contributions of art to individuals' lives, and its social significance. Part of this learning has to do with the importance of
imagination to artistic production and interpretation.

As well as revealing our uniqueness, our imaginations tie each of
us to other human beings. For example, native populations in North
America and Australia consider dream states to be critical to making
and interpreting art. Australian Aboriginals and some Native American tribal groups value the imagery derived from dreams, which are
considered a form of cultural symbolism. Although dream images also
involve personal symbols, the collective imaginations of these social
groups are a foundation for artistic imagery; old symbols mix with new
and group feelings mix with the personal as imagination becomes the
storehouse for, and a medium in which visual culture is created and
interpreted.

Imagination develops through interdisciplinary and disciplinary
experiences with visual culture, which are contexts that play a
part in the extension of meaning and learning. Visual culture influences
people's interests, but also changes based on imaginative vizualization
in response to interests. For example, sports fashion has changed as new
sports have become popular, including becoming popular to new groups,
such as when women began to ride bicycles in the 19th century. Although it can be argued that people can only artistically realize their
imaginative creations through knowledge of form and materials, such
knowledge is useless without ideas, attitudes, beliefs, and emotions.
As will be discussed in Chapter 3, the contexts of visual culture are
important to extending meaning and promoting learning.

Form and Extended Meanings

Of course, form is critical to visual culture; it is the immediacy and seductiveness of form that makes visual culture so powerful. The problem of curriculum is not form, it is an overreliance on formalism in education. To conceptualize aesthetics in curriculum as only formalist or expressionist does not do justice to the complexity of visual culture. However, in contrast to mainstream curriculum, which tends to establish a border conflict, *form versus meaning*, in an increasing body of contemporary theory, *meaning is inherent to aesthetics* and interested interpretations are not only expected, but promoted. Postmodern artists often reject formalistic uses of the elements and principles of design in favor of symbolic uses that suggest multiple and extended social meanings. As will be discussed in Chapter 4, extended meanings made by students enrich their learning.

Consider two examples of the problem of teaching from a formalistic perspective that cross the borders of fine art and popular culture. In the piece *Us-Them* by Gary Simmons, the artist uses two black towels hanging on a rack, one with the word "Us" embroidered on it in gold, and the other with the word "Them" to suggest meaning. Simmons refers to the typically white-colored "His" and "Hers" towels, which are associated with wealth, but changes an element (the color) from white to black, which symbolically references the many meanings people have of these colors and changes the text to "Us" and "Them." He juxtaposes color with ideas of elitism, gender, and social conflict suggested by the objects and words, so that the color black suggests the word (black) and the word suggests and combines with knowledge, feelings, and beliefs about racial tension. In other words, Simmons does not use color for formal reasons, and as a result, formalism would not go a long way in helping students gain access to the piece. Instead, color is a sign that extends meaning by suggesting associations based on the audience's experience.

Simmons counts on both diverse and common cultural knowledge of his audience to provide a vehicle for the construction of meaning. He works at the boundary of different types of visual culture to suggest interpretations that borrow from each. The references function in multiple ways depending on the audience. I have discussed Simmons' work with students in other countries who interpreted it as a statement about "the U.S." and all the other countries of the world.

Cindy Sherman's work of the 1980s references other connections between forms of visual culture: fine art photographs, popular films, and pornography. It suggests to us movies we have seen, images that are retained in our memories, some that may only be recalled through the references of her work. Her work is powerful in its ability to force us to use what we have learned from imagery, including things that we may not like to admit are part of our knowledge store. It confronts and challenges our accepted representations of ourselves, as social beings, as women and men, as audiences, and so on. Like Simmons's work, we create Sherman's work through our knowledge of popular culture and the new meanings that become attached to her imagery as we come to see it as fine art. Sherman references and points to fictions that suggest social realities.

Contemporary Views: The New Aesthetics

Even into the late 20th century, aesthetics was discussed in terms of a relatively naïve general audience; however, no audience in a postindustrial democracy can be considered visually naïve. Postmodern visual culture, such as popular films that have postmodern forms (e.g., *Brazil*, *Pulp Fiction*, *Clockwork Orange*, *Eyes Wide Shut*, *Orlando*) are edited in a pastiche that focuses the audience on structure and process, which takes away the possibility of an easy linear narrative; it challenges even the notion of a narrative by making us pay attention to cuts and camera angles. These films overtly draw on our cognitive connections, sometimes deliberately confusing us, and demand that we reference other cultural experiences in order to make meaning. These films do not have to *tell* a story—we construct stories for the filmmakers—and because common film stories have become so familiar, it is the confusion that keeps our interest (we try to "figure it out") and the images, editing, and other artistic techniques.

The search for new conceptions of aesthetics appropriate to contemporary visual culture requires an educational reconsideration of applications of formalism and crossing boundaries such as between "high" and "low" art. However, these challenges are not new. Critical theorists connected to the Frankfurt School of sociology helped prepare the way, although still maintaining a clear distinction between high and low culture. Aesthetician Theodore Adorno understood that the critical issue was formalistic as he lamented the collapse of the boundaries between fine art and popular culture. Adorno stated in a letter to Walter Benjamin in response to the latter's *The Work of Art in the Age of Mechanical Reproduction*,

> I agree with you that the aural element of the work of art is declining—not only because of its technical reproducibility, incidentally, but above all because of the fulfillment of its own "autonomous" formal laws . . . (Adorno, 1936/1992)

Adorno made the point. The importance of formal relationships is firmly established and it is a contradiction to claim that these relationships are trivial. But it is important to understand that it is the focus on formal attributes of the visual arts that have resulted in the collapsing of categories of visual culture. To try to maintain the idea that fine art is inherently different from the other visual arts, while at the same time understanding that connections between the visual arts are found in their forms, is a contradiction that has caused a disjuncture in education and culture.

Postmodern theorists tend to concur with Habermas (1987) that a distinction between the premodern and modern periods is the idea of the modern to create itself from itself without revisiting the past. It is in the question of whether this is possible, and the extent to which the idea is favorable, where disagreement exists. In contrast, postmodern visual culture and aesthetic theory deliberately recycle the past. Aestheticians who might be considered postmodern, such as Zygmunt Bauman (1993), Paul Crowther (1993), Hilde Hein (1993), Peter McCormick (1990), and Richard Shusterman (1992), consider revisiting the past and rereading texts that have been ignored to be an imperative precisely because they did not fit neatly into these conditions of mainstream, modern philosophy.

Aesthetician Paul Crowther (1993) argues that the beginning of modernism can be found in the new patterns of production of the industrial revolution. A division of labor is the foundation of modern, efficient practice. From the work of Kant, different forms of knowledge and experience became increasingly thought of as separate from one another. Metaphysical thinking was considered distinct from scientific method and aesthetic experience was conceptualized as separate from ethical judgment. That is, the aesthetic good was not necessarily the ethical right, which was of critical importance at the time because it allowed for art to emerge as separate from church and court and is fundamental to contemporary understandings of art in democratic societies. However, the extreme (high modernist) interpretation of the idea resulted in a definition of the aesthetic good that did more than not require reference to the ethical good; it did not allow references to ethical issues.

Contemporary art, media, and literary theory tends to focus more on the suggestiveness of signs and the ways in which meaning is constructed by audiences than on only formal qualities per se or artist personal self-expression. In contrast to the earlier view—that an author or artist controls the message that will be taken from his or her work—response theory begins with the assumption that each member of an audience constructs his or her own meaning. Based on hermeneutics, this perspective of audience involvement attends to the interpretation of literary and visual texts dependent on individual, lived experience.

As part of the process of teaching visual culture in its complexity, new methods and sources of information have been introduced into the academy, such as oral histories, ethnographic studies, and computer-based forms of research that allow large quantities of data to be analyzed and interpreted. Some visual cultural traditions, such as those of the folk arts, are best studied through interpersonal contacts and studies of the recent past of computer gaming can be done through anonymous interviews on the Internet. In the process, sources of information once considered inappropriate for use in academic study are becoming understood as helpful to teaching and learning. New methods of study allow new questions to be asked, just as new questions lead to new methods, and through these questions a better understanding of the relationships between forms of visual culture and their social relevance can emerge.

Crossing Cultural Borders

Generically conceptualizing the visual culture of individual cultures, subcultures, or professional communities as completely separate is no more helpful than universalizing them. It is no longer easy to view cultures or subcultures as totally separate because they interact on many levels and through many media. Fine artists borrow imagery from popular culture, men borrow from women, artists in the United States borrow from other countries, and so on. We have only to look at the work of Pop artists who show in museums and also design advertisements, feature films and product lines based on cartoons, and objects appropriated from native cultures to be placed in natural history museums in some instances and art museums in others.

The capacity of form to produce some predictable emotional responses in people who share common cultures is a good example of the tie between shape and content. This capacity enables form to heighten or reduce the relative significance of content; form can make trivial content appear significant, and the significant seem trivial. Some forms suggest a range of common meanings, but the emphasis of those meanings may be different to different groups of people. This is illustrated by Lorna Simpson's work *Wigs* in Figure 2.1, which suggests a range of common meanings having to do with visual culture articles of beauty and more specific meanings concerning group identities.

Because people with different backgrounds and interests do not have the same foundations for interpretation and will experience the same

Figure 2.1. Lorna Simpson, *Wigs*. 1995. Waterless lithograph on felt.

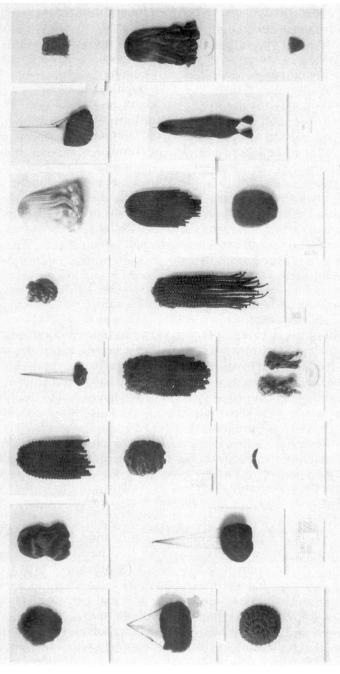

Collection Walker Art Center, Minneapolis. T.B. Walker Acquistion Fund, 1995.

visual culture in different ways, the value of visual culture changes from one cultural context to another (e.g., Anderson, 1990; Coote & Shelton, 1992; Layton, 1991). As a result, the application of the same aesthetic models to all art would be inappropriate. Aboriginal dot paintings and postmodern art both exemplify the problem: Each can be looked at formally, but in most cases, neither will be interpreted in its richest sense from that perspective. Although a painting of a mother and child may result in cross-cultural interpretations by viewers, particular interpretations will depend on sex, religion, and many other aspects of viewing.

In education, form requires many types of discussion and will have greater or lesser importance depending on the work and what viewers bring to the work. For example, the elements and principles of design can be discussed from at least a symbolic, organizational, emotional, perceptual, or technical perspective. Different age groups will be able to address aesthetic issues at different levels and artistic styles will be interpreted differently at different ages. Figure 2.2 illustrates alternative Western conceptions of aesthetics that integrate form with meaning and which have contributed to emerging postmodern positions. Alternative perspectives on form also exist in different cultures.

AESTHETICS AND THE CONSTRUCTION OF MEANING: PRAGMATIST AND NEOPRAGMATIST VIEWS

The construction of meaning has always been vital to visual culture, but it has not always been reflected as so in education. As John Dewey (1916/1944) wrote in 1916 in *Democracy and Education*:

> It is frequently stated that a person learns by merely having the qualities of things impressed upon his mind through the gateway of the senses. Having received a store of sensory impressions, association or some power of mental synthesis is supposed to combine them into ideas—into things with a *meaning* . . . The difference between an adjustment to a physical stimulus and a *mental* act is that the latter involves response to a thing in its *meaning*; the former does not . . . When things have a meaning to us, we *mean* (intend, propose) what we do: when they do not, we act blindly, unconsciously, unintelligently. (emphasis in original, p. 29)

The notion that aesthetic experience is something set apart from daily life and experience was rejected by Dewey (1934). He viewed art as fundamentally providing an integrative experience connecting body and mind and criticized the idea of an aesthetic that sought to separate the two. Although the peculiar characteristic of art is its form,

Figure 2.2. Conceptual form: Alternative approaches for teaching visual culture.

SYMBOLISM	The approach to aesthetics in which form is conceptualized as having symbolic significance
EXPRESSIONISM	The aesthetic argument that form inherently promotes human expression of emotion
FORM FOLLOWS FUNCTION	The Bauhaus perspective of form as being in the service of use
GESTALT	The position put forth most comprehensively by Arnheim that the context of form is critical to its perception and immediate interpretation
MEDIUM AS MESSAGE	McLuhan's argument that a medium or form is a mediator and extension of human meanings
PRAGMATISM	Originally Dewey's account of aesthetics conceptualized as inherently educational and a part of social experience
FORMALISM	From Bell's turn-of-the-20th-century book; based on the argument that art can be universally understood in terms of form as form
POSTMODERNISM	The argument that form may be appropriately interpreted in many ways, but that contexts are important to interpretation

Dewey did not conceptualize form as a vehicle through which one could have a purely ethereal encounter. Rather, awareness of form attunes us to the psychobiological conditions of being human and our senses work together to promote aesthetic connections, enriching our experience of form.

For Dewey, art was part of the natural state of the world and the union of fine art and life was vital. He viewed art as the extreme expression of the relationship between material, process, and idea. As such, art was created from human desire and embodied the realization of the interaction between people and their environment. According to Dewey, art was a reason for living.

Dewey's focus was on the interaction of process, product, and the social aspects of artistic experience, not just free self-expression or individual artist intent. His perspective of art as experience involved a cycle of communication resulting from making and viewing. He was acutely aware of the importance of social context to that experience and denied the common assumption of many of his contempories on art that great works of art have inherent, universal qualities that make them great. Dewey explained that art is made as a result of something "occasional, something having its own date and place" (p. 109). Rather than being universal, art that continues to be valued over time is valued because it is experienced in new ways by different people at different times.

Dewey understood art as inherently educational, but complained that common educational methods prohibited the use of art in general instruction. He saw these methods as distinct from the means of instruction that art could facilitate because they did not take into account imagination and emotion. Such an interpretation meant that art was to be infused in curriculum so that all subject areas were influenced by it. From Dewey's perspective, students were to get an aesthetic education, not merely an art education.

In contrast to Dewey's hopes, the focus of school art practice became production separate from aesthetic appreciation, in part due to the focus on schooling for vocational skills. Dewey's ideas about the social qualities of art learning and art knowledge were translated in a highly individualistic way, which was consistent with the individualism that increasingly dominated the fine art community and education as the 1930s drew to a close and an emphasis on individual responsibility for social and economic conditions became part of national, political discourse. This focus involved a neglect of the social aspects of art that Dewey considered a vital part of artistic and aesthetic experience. It also involved conflicts of conscience as educators became enmeshed in the problems of the relationship between child and adult art, evaluation of children's artistic expression, an increasing national interest in personality and talent testing, and standards of judgment and taste. Although Dewey's direct influence on American public schooling has long been debated, since this period, general education has had increasing responsibility for the social aspects of children's development. And yet, the form of production that perhaps most suggests and reflects social life has been endangered in education.

Dewey was responding to academic and metaphysical positions against which science could be used to argue in favor of a more humane educational practice. At that time, the academy represented a closed system of control and narrowly defined rules. So, the rejection of the academic and the metaphysical by Dewey (in favor of the "scientific") was a rejection of an old, institutional perspective, in favor of a new, experiential view.

Dewey's work is one of the keys to finding the intersection of aesthetics, contemporary visual culture, and education. It suggests that curriculum has an artistic form, which can borrow from scientific inquiry while aiding (in part, through the self-reflective character of art) our understanding of what is lacking in the science of teaching. It focuses attention on both the educational and aesthetic aspects of experience.

Dewey's ideas, which have been largely ignored by aestheticians of the past, are now being revisited by neopragmatists like Richard Shusterman, a contemporary aesthetician. Shusterman (1992) locates pragmatist aesthetics between analytic and continental aesthetics in order to draw on the empirical sense of the former and the broad, sociocultural perspective of the latter. I have always been uncomfortable with the apparently elitist perspective of Adorno's aesthetic, which has been a foundation for much continental theory, and yet, American analytic aesthetics is debilitating from an educational standpoint, in its limiting of the power of art to its "internal," especially formal, qualities. Shusterman's work helps to form a link between the Anglo-American and continental traditions by seeking to explain lived aesthetic experience in a contemporary democracy.

Shusterman's argument is based on the relationship between popular and "high" culture. He is seeking an experiential aesthetic that describes the way in which people interact with different forms of visual culture in the same way and argues that by focusing on the actual experience people have with popular cultural objects, we can see a relationship between the two. Drawing on media studies, he reminds us that audiences create their own meanings when responding to culture, which in turn act upon cultural forms. In contrast to the opinion of Pierre Bourdieu, who has studied the sociological conditions of artistic forms, Shusterman argues that fine art is not autonomous.

To further his argument, such interactions occur in and through the medium of the social world with which Dewey was concerned. Neopragmatism leads us to a social aesthetic that is dependent on education—not so that people can appreciate fine art, but so that they can gain access to the multiple meanings of visual culture.

CONCLUSION

Art is not only about the isolated effects of formal qualities, and several aesthetic theories exist that can and should be drawn upon in teaching. In an increasing body of contemporary theory, meaning is inherent to aesthetic experience, and in contemporary visual culture and aes-

thetic theory interested interpretations are not only expected, but promoted. As exemplified above, postmodern artists often reject formalistic uses of the elements and principles of design in favor of symbolic
uses that suggest multiple and extended social meanings. As minimalist
artists have taught us, form is never pure; it can always stimulate associations. Postmodern conceptions of aesthetics, then, involve a social
relationship between people mediated by visual culture. Dewey was
right—we come to know art through the dynamics of experience—but
experience has changed.

CHAPTER 3

The Social Life of Art

The Importance of Connecting the Past with the Present

CONNECTIONS BETWEEN CONTEMPORARY VISUAL CULTURE and the past are critically important if students are to develop an understanding of the complexity of their visual world. Part of this complexity involves the ways in which the past lives in the present and future. For example, *ofrendas* (altars) and *stanos* (icons) represent living histories. They are integrated into people's daily lives through religious beliefs and through the recycling of their related images and objects. Educators' consciousness of the importance of these connections has broadened as a result of inquiry into the range and influence of cultural traditions on present-day life and the need for students to improve their knowledge of traditions. The educational challenge of teaching visual culture of the past is not merely a matter of teaching art history, but rather the bigger issue of helping students to develop an understanding of the rich social life of visual culture.

In order to meet this challenge, this chapter focuses on three topics. First, a critical examination of the discipline of art history will help to frame the discussion about teaching visual culture of the past. Second, the importance of contexts and a reconsideration of judgments of quality for teaching will be discussed. Third, relationships between past, present, and future in postmodern visual culture will be considered.

THE OLD AND THE NEW ART HISTORIES

Studying history helps us to understand the cultures and societies that provide us with the conceptual locations we now inhabit and illustrates the limits and possibilities of human behavior. However, history is not the past; it is the reconstruction of the past. Because the past is made up of people and events to which we no longer have direct access, history involves interpretations of remnants of those events and the objects created by those people.

The discipline of mainstream art history is made up of stories, based on evidence, that reflect the moment in which they are written as much as they reflect the past. Art history is grounded in the serious and thoughtful research of selected objects, but it generally gives little attention to larger social, political, and economic concerns that are the contexts of artistic production. In fact, some of the most sophisticated analyses of contexts of art (e.g., Bourdieu, 1984; Hauser, 1974/1982; see also During, 1993; Grossberg, Nelson, & Treichner, 1992 for anthologies) are called "social history" or not considered part of the discipline at all because they address those complex concerns.

Art historian Donald Preziosi (1989) points out that

> art history worked to make the synoptically visible so that it might function in and upon the present: so that the present might be seen as the demonstrable *product* of a particular past; and so that the past so staged might be framed as an *object of historical desire*; figured from which a modern citizen might desire descent. (p. 18, ital. in original)

As such, the discipline of art history has cast what came to be called the fine arts in a role of elevated economic value, moral virtue, and universal appreciation. Preziosi further states, "The principle product of art history has thus been modernity itself" (p. 18).

Social contexts are critical to the work of some art historians, classified as social historians, suggesting that social contexts are not an essential part of the mainstream focus of art history. However, Preziosi (1989) argues that the social historian is "concerned with the signs of the various roles played by artwork in simultaneously generating, sustaining, and reflecting broader, social, cultural and historical processes" (p. 12) and represents one of three major perspectives in the field. The other two are the perspective "of the *connoisseur*, involved in delineating the minute signs of biographic and temporal identity, a semiological task of great skill; [and] that of the *iconographer*, involved in the semiological task of delineating networks of signifiers and signifieds and their morphological and referential transformations over time and place" (p. 12, italics added). However, only one of these perspectives tends to be emphasized in curriculum (other than for art historians), and it is usually most akin to connoisseurship.

The idea of connoisseurship has been around for centuries, but the large-scale influence of the method did not begin until the 19th century with the emergence of the professional field. The connoisseur was believed to have both special sensitivities and highly developed specialized skills for appraising art based on technical attributes of the work. In the early 20th century, connoisseurs tended to be collectors or helped collectors make good investments. They were taught to use particular parts of a painting, such as an ear or a nose, to identify an artist (Berenson, 1902). Connoisseurs concerned themselves with finding out facts about when a work of art was made and who made it in order to understand at what level of appreciation (both aesthetic and financial) it should be valued.

The defining boundaries of art history have not typically extended to popular forms of art, art made by people of non-Western cultures, or even some cross-cultural aspects of Western fine art. In fact, popular visual arts and mass media images are considered unrelated to art history to such an extent that they tend to be studied in different departments at universities, such as cultural studies, anthropology, communications, or media studies. These different professional communities have each claimed certain aspects of the knowledge associated with images and objects and represent those aspects as more different than similar, in order it reify disciplinary boundaries and maintain distinctions between the professional practices that are the foundations of those boundaries. As a result, the processes of historical study of popular visual culture are often closer to those of etymology or archeology than of art history. And, in order to understand the production and use of visual culture in diverse cultural contexts we often go to those other disciplines, or outside professional disciplines altogether, because these are better sources of sociocultural information. For example, we would have to seek information about the mass production of cultural products, even those involving reproductions of fine art, from sociological studies of industry.

The professional discipline of art history has been crafted over centuries, beginning at least in the 16th century with Giorgio Vasari's *Lives of the Artists*, to focus on debates about the canons of art and discussions about the people working within those canons. In part, these debates stemmed from such arbitrary roots as attempts made centuries ago to distinguish between the virtues of Italian Renaissance art and those of the art of Northern Europe (Gombrich, 1966). As art historian Steve Edwards (1998) explains:

> What is significant here, however, is that ways of making and thinking about art that were developed within a particular set of historical priori-

ties have acquired a general character. . . . It is even possible that the focus, in the canon of twentieth-century art, on French painting with its preference for harmony, balance, and order rather than the work produced in, say, Berlin or Moscow (based on very different "tastes"), is the outcome of just these long-running patterns of preference. (p. 4) . . . The canon is a structural condition for art history. (p. 23)

Many of the historical roots of Euro-American visual culture can be found in European crafts and go back at least to Elizabethan England. However, the European, ideological foundations of contemporary popular culture can be found earlier in writings about trade and the craft guilds of the Middle Ages (Lucie-Smith, 1981), aspects of which are included in the history of fine art. Also, many forms of contemporary popular culture and fine art have multicultural and cross-cultural roots and crossed interdisciplinary paths of scientific and technological development.

Similar to Clive Bell's (1913) attempt to relate representational and abstract art through formalism, art historian Heinrich Wölfflin (1915/1950) recommended several formal and dichotomous concepts (such as painterly versus linear, plane versus depth, and closed versus open form) as categories of analysis. These and other art historical categories, such as art styles, have since influenced the general discourse about art in education.

Educational experiences with the range of visual culture are not so easily categorized. We experience and study visual culture in many ways; even when we attempt to limit our study of it to a historical canon, we must go outside of art history for appropriate language and other aids to analysis.

The methods of valuation developed by art historians have influenced the ways in which educated people think about art. Even the works of art that are reproduced in books, slides, films, and so on, and are therefore available for classroom use, have often been selected as important by art historians. Most teachers of at least baby-boomer age got their basic art history education through standard texts, such as H. W. Janson's book *History of Art*, and the "art in the dark" teaching method. Janson's text, which has been notoriously lacking in social and cultural connections, is an example of traditional, mainstream art history. Such texts neglect the lessons of European "social historians" such as Arnold Hauser (e.g., 1974/1982, 1985). They have also lacked examples of art by women and men of color. Feminist art historians have criticized such surveys of Western art, and some work has been done toward changing these texts. However, professors and K–12 teachers on the whole still must supplement these books with additional readings, on women artists, for example, which unfortunately may work to reify the separation of the groups they seek to include.

New Histories in Curriculum

The new art history is quite different from the old art history. Less important is the narrow influence of individual objects and styles on subsequent fine art and more important are the social influences and dynamics of cultural development. It shifts attention away from connoisseurship as the basic method of teaching about the past in art education.

Art historians have questioned their discipline from several perspectives, perhaps most strongly from the perspective of representations of art. For example, in *Vision and Painting: The Logic of the Gaze*, art historian Norman Bryson (1983) argues against E. H. Gombrich's claim that painting is essentially a record of perception. Bryson notes that it is understandable why Gombrich would make such as argument based on early views of aesthetics and the history of Western art. However, he challenges his field by pointing out that "viewing is an activity of transforming the material of paintings into meanings, and that transformation is perpetual, nothing can arrest it" (p. xiv). This challenges the old view of art history as the discipline that seeks to discover the meaning of art of the past as a single, perceived (rather than conceived) reality.

Bryson's vision for art history is to understand paintings as signs and the process of painting as a form of social production. In rejecting Gombrich's view of individual perception, he is careful not to fall into the trap of Sassure's semiotics, with its focus on formal constraints. Rather, Bryson and other culture historians who work in the realm of the visual arts (e.g., Bogart, 1995; Leppert, 1996; Preziosi, 1989) discuss painting as a mediation system in flux that is continually and inherently about the production of multiple meanings.

Other art historians have challenged representations of art in their field as built on a foundation of historicism, which is modernist, colonialist, and chronological (Preziosi, 1989). Historicism is based on the idea of evolutionary cultural development, which assumes that the story of the past is linear and progressive. Critical contemporary art historians suggest that this chronology—which is an accumulation of relatively isolated events—has in some ways inhibited understandings of the past; for example, it has limited an appreciation of the profound consequences of influence by certain social, gender, and cultural groups.

Concepts of Time/Space

Art history is taught in relation to certain interpretations of the concept of time, and the most typical of these interpretations is represented by a timeline, shaped by the historicism discussed above. From this perspective, actions and events seem to be discrete bits of time, independent of the historical and cultural frameworks that make them possible, and outside the multidimensional medium of time and space that suspends them. This is problematic because the representation carries with it an assumption that the past is linear and atomistic, made up of actions and reactions, and as if peoples and ideas that are off the timeline do not exist. Western art history survey is only one of many possible contexts in which to present art of the past; and yet, it is by far the most commonly taught in the United States. Using a survey timeline to teach history seriously underrepresents important aspects of the past, in part because it limits our ability to conceptualize relationships between and across cultures. Origins of art and periods of style are often shown as if arbitrarily determined and not represented as if they are part of larger cultural change.

An alternative perspective of time is to focus on long periods of time as historical structures of consciousness (Braudel, 1980). Structure dictates certain constants over time, providing people with, and being reflected in, collective subjectivities or ways of thinking. Sociohistorical structure tends toward similarity over time by shaping the consciousness of individuals, who then influence others. In part, the influence occurs through the maintenance of values and ideals, such as individualism, embedded in the structure. At the same time, structure contains contradictions and disjunctures, which provide the elements of transformation.

From this perspective, time is represented as a multidimensional space, rather than a line, which various cultural groups inhabit and influence as their ideas coexist and collide. This interpretation gives attention to the important connections between moments and consciousness, as well as between actions and reactions. Time is no longer represented as if it is in isolation from other critical aspects of the past, and an education in visual culture becomes the study of heritage and identity. Multidimensional representations of the past, such as time-spaces (three-dimensional timelines), genealogical trees, and time arts

animations can convey historical relationships between cultures better than the sole use of timelines.

Teaching the new art history, which involves greater attention to
social and cultural issues, is difficult in institutions of higher education and in secondary schools for a number of reasons (Gormally &
Nunn, 1988). Although most art students are female, most higher education faculty are male and still teach a patriarchal version of art history. The structure of faculty positions limits the teaching of new
perspectives as a result of curriculum problems, such as generally accepted course titles and textbooks, and students have expectations that
are contrary to the new visions of the field. Also, narrow and conservative standardized tests make new knowledge extremely difficult to
present.

Much of what we teach are remnants of knowledge. Through the
process of teaching, sense is made of these many, often decontextualized
and sometimes conflicting, bits of information. Therefore, it is important to teach as much as possible in ways that help to rebuild contexts
of the past by connecting these bits in relevant and meaningful ways.
In order to do this, contexts must be connected to student learning
outside, as well as inside, of school.

CONTEXTS AND QUALITY

Contexts of production and viewing play a large part in determinations
of whether particular forms, images, and objects of visual culture are
considered worthy academic subject material. The importance of visual
culture is, in part, influenced by the central role that visual fine art has
played historically in the ways we see and represent our world, but it
has also been influenced by other visual forms that have crossed over
and outside of arts disciplines. An education in visual culture must be
thought of from interdisciplinary and extradisciplinary positions that
allow information from inside and outside of school to be connected to
school subjects.

The Importance of Production and Viewing Contexts

Context actually means *contexts*, because no image or object has only
one context. As Gestalt psychologist Rudolph Arnheim (1974), who is
noted for his studies of the perceptual analysis of visual form, pointed
out, "All aspects of the mind bear on art, be they cognitive, social, or
motivational" (p. 4). At least two broad categories of contexts can be

differentiated: *production contexts* (artists and milieu) and *viewing contexts* (viewers and milieu).

Production contexts are situations in which visual culture is created. When studying a particular image or object, production contexts include theory, such as aesthetic theory, that influenced the artist, as well as personal history and social milieu. For decades, sociologists have understood that the contexts of art and other cultural carriers contribute to their symbolic, attached meanings (Berger & Luckmann, 1967). Such contexts also include the conditions and environments that make student art possible, from what students see every day to sources of their emotions, opinions, and beliefs.

Viewing contexts are environments in which visual culture is seen and used. These include classrooms, theaters, museums, galleries, television, or magazines in which visual culture is experienced. They also include aesthetic theories, theories about childhood, and other ideas that shape our viewing. But, perhaps even more important, viewing contexts are dependent upon viewers' individual and collective imagic stores. The imagic store is the collection of allusive images that people hold in memory (Broudy, 1987). Broudy demonstrated that the rich development of this store is critically important to general education because it makes possible the comprehension of the allusions to the arts. Our imagic store not only enables us to understand references to images; it also enables us to build on past knowledge and create new images and objects. As such it is integral to the educational and human experience. Experiential contexts develop in the minds of people as they view images. Arnheim (1974) stated,

> Every visual experience is embedded in a context of space and time. Just as the appearance of objects is influenced by that of neighboring objects in space, so also it is influenced by sights that preceded it in time. (p. 50)

A good example of the influence of viewing contexts was the collection and display of modernist masterpieces (including works by Monet, Van Gogh, Degas, and Picasso) by multimillionaire Steve Wynn in his Las Vegas casino Bellagio. The question denoting what might be a typical public response was asked by art critic Robert Hughes (1999):

> Why should the idea of starting an art collection in Las Vegas seem so odd? Basically because Las Vegas—the Disney World of terminal public greed—is a city in which every cultural citation is fake, so that the real thing feels out of place. The city is built on simulation, quotation, weird unconvincing displacements, in which cultural icons are endlessly but never convincingly quoted. (p. 51)

The idea of displaying great art in a Las Vegas casino should not seem at all odd to us after continually seeing fine art recycled, transposed, and transfixed with new meanings as an increasingly vital (and normal) part of contemporary culture. To view this art is to add to the meaning it suggests from previous associations with high culture with the casino atmosphere, which is one of spending, luck, and fortune.

From this perspective, context is not peripheral to visual culture, or any given work of art; it is a part of visual culture. Contexts provide the conceptual connections that make images and objects worthy of study and is as much a part of a work of art as its form, function, or symbolic meaning. It is a type of narrative loosely attached to the physical object, as is a story portrayed by its image. Although such narratives are attached to a work of art in the ways in which symbolic meaning is attached to certain forms, they are also interpreted. As a result, in new contexts, responses to visual culture are not only formed, they are *trans*formed. Some artists even reify contexts by overtly including them in their work through explanatory text or planning sketches. As discussed in Chapter 2, the transformative power of contemporary visual culture exemplifies the ways in which aesthetics is now conceptualized as tied at its foundation to experience and meaning.

Judgments of Quality

In part, distinctions between various forms of visual culture have been based on social politics and gender differences. Design historian Penny Sparke (1995) has argued that as industrialization advanced and the middle class grew, women became increasingly responsible for making the home a haven for men's comfort and a display of men's wealth. Women were the purveyors of taste and had the work of making textiles and other products used in the home. By the mid- to late 19th century, a movement was afoot in Great Britain and the United States to make a change. Men such as John Ruskin and Henry Cole, director of the South Kensington Museum, worked to separate good taste from bad, claiming that bad taste was in the home. Good taste could be found in men's institutions, particularly museums, art academies, and design schools.

During the 20th century, modernistic aesthetics were used to support judgments of quality that promoted distinctions between fine art and popular visual culture. For example, mid-century cultural theorist Leo Lowenthal (1950/1959) wrote about the ongoing debate between culture and leisure as a crisis between "high" and "low" culture. He discussed the problem of people paying too much attention to popular culture and stated the general public concern about its ill effects. He asserted that the opposite of popular culture is art, arguing that:

> today artistic products are losing the character of spontaneity more and more and are being replaced by the phenomena of popular culture, which are nothing but a manipulated reproduction of reality as it is; and, in so doing, popular culture sanctions and glorifies whatever it finds worth echoing. (p. 49)

Lowenthal was discussing radio.

By the mid-20th century, the separation between popular visual culture and fine art became overtly political. It was supported by the rejection of fascist art and propaganda and by the political distinctions between the United States and the Soviet Union. As discussed in Chapter 2, art critic Clement Greenberg labeled Soviet socialist realism ideological kitsch and contrasted its analysis with what he claimed was a nonideological, formalist analysis of fine art (1946/1959). However, the underlying problems of claims that Soviet art was political and American art was not have since been revealed and the claims have been demonstrated to be, at least in part, the political embodiment of McCarthy-era mentality (Guilbaud, 1984). These Cold War politics shaped the emergence of international marketing of American art and culture. Today, the growing literature of contemporary art theory not only demonstrates the ways in which all art is political, but also the underlying ideological assumptions of the denial of politics as inherent to art.

As boundaries between various forms of visual culture break down, old assumptions of quality must be interrogated, quality in curriculum content must be redefined, and instructional methods must be reconsidered in relation to contemporary experience. Quality can no longer be determined by virtue of the fact that a work or a form of visual culture is seen in museums or that it functions as cultural capital in elite circles. Even the notion of what constitutes cultural capital has expanded with popular culture tied to newer technologies, so that the well-educated may be as well-versed in website design as they are in classical music, interior design, or fashion.

Differences between the study of art history and the history of other visual culture are fundamentally tied to the different purposes visual culture has fulfilled for its makers and viewers. These purposes are not as discrete as is often assumed. As discussed in Chapter 2, an assumption has existed that fine art is intended to be appraised and appreciated for disinterested, aesthetic purposes. However, feminist theorists and historians have cautioned us that the male view of a nude female figure will likely be a gendered gaze and, as media study experts have pointed out, the seductive influence of aesthetic appreciation informs of the purposes of advertisers.

An important issue at the root of teaching art is the issue of quality. In the recent past, quality in curriculum content has typically referred to the problem of deciding which exemplars to include in instruction. Issues of quality centered on the selection of objects rather than the selection of critical concepts. A fundamental assumption and line of argument on which this tradition has been based is that the only art worth teaching is "good" art and good art contains and conveys "goodness" (such as elevated values, conventional design qualities, craftsmanship). Goodness in fine art has been determined by, for example, the elevating quality of a piece or its influence on artistic style.

Even the term *art* has traditionally signified a judgment of quality. The term has been used in education to represent something inherently good; in fact, the term *art* carries with it assumptions of quality, value, and enrichment. However, the visual arts are not *inherently* good in their effects. The great power of the visual arts is their ability to have various and profound effects on our lives, but that power can also make them manipulative, colonizing, and disenfranchising. Visual culture that is considered good for one group may hurt others and the complexity of this relationship needs to be considered as part of educational experience.

This is a serious problem from the standpoint of teaching visual culture, because most of the visual arts that students see are not particularly elevating, and much of the "elevating" art from the past elevated some people above others (that is, it was considered good, at least in part, because it reified the "value" of some people more than others). The fact is that not all art is good for us—or rather, any type of art may be good or bad for us—and the bad qualities of art should be addressed in school, just as should the good qualities. Good historical art is easy for teachers to talk about and assess (we already know it is "good"); it has "stood the test of time" and been talked and written about many times. But this definition of quality does not help us in determining quality in and on the borders of contemporary fine art and popular culture, which is one important reason why little new visual culture is addressed in classrooms. The problem is that much of the art judged to be good by the old criteria is at best only indirectly connected to, and at worst is irrelevant to, the cross-cultural, interdisciplinary, multimodal experiences of students' daily lives.

Visual culture is a form of social production; it plays an important role in the construction of social life. It mediates between people who communicate social ideas through it in social contexts. Therefore, visual culture is worth teaching if it is powerful—if it influences the way people think about the world, visualize, and live in it. In order to deal with the issue of quality in an educational context, we must ask, What art is worth teaching? (which is not the same question as, What art is good?) and ask, What about art is most important to learn? From an educational standpoint, we can conceptualize quality not as great (inherent) value, but as powerful (social) influence.

The Importance of Context to Making Judgments

Teaching from this perspective does not mean teaching in a relativistic manner and it is inappropriate to say that presenting popular culture and multicultural art in education suggests a lowering of standards or a lack of concern for quality. Quite the contrary—to teach a work of art out of context suggests that no judgments of quality have been made and that "anything goes." Contexts are defined by social groups and cultures that each have an internal logic and complex systems of checks and balances for determining quality within the group. To contextualize learning is to help students understand that many conditions influence judgments of goodness and that those judgments are made based on the relationship of these conditions.

Research indicates that an understanding of context is a higher level of thinking than students achieve when instructed in only studio techniques and processes (e.g., Erickson, 1998; Short, 1998). According to this research, study of the past helps students to interpret unfamiliar works of art. When students do not have contextual information, they construct their own contexts. For example, in one study students discussed a painting of two Eastern Indian gods as if it represented an interracial couple (Freedman & Wood, 1999). The students had not been informed that an ideal aesthetic of a single racial couple was represented in the painting. Lighter skin was considered aesthetically pleasing for women and darker skin was desired for men at the time and place the painting was created. Instead, the lack of understanding of this critical aspect of the painting was interpreted by the students in relation to their own context.

When we study visual culture of the past, we look at it in at least two ways. One way is through our own past. That is, we look at it through our perspective of an object coming to us from the past through our interest in learning, collecting, being challenged, being entertained, and so on. The second way we look at visual culture is through the eyes of historians and other professionals who create the culture of history. That is, we seek out and allow people who have studied the past to teach us facts and interpretations. Although it is likely that a professional historian will have the deepest, richest knowledge of the past, both the professional views of present-day historians and our own, personal and/ or lay views are contemporary views of the past; both are derived from contemporary passions.

Cultural historian Richard Leppert (1996) discusses what happens when different sources of visual culture information cross paths and bits of the past become part of the present. Leppert uses the example of the knowledge he has gained about tulips from his historical investigations of Dutch painting and his personal experience with the flowers. He explains:

> The tulip's beauty-quotient came at the price of moral qualms, and even guilt, over the monies being spent in Holland to obtain real tulips—ironically, far more than might be spent on a painting of a tulip in many instances—and for that matter, over the materialism implicit in the purchase of paintings themselves. Indeed flower paintings belonged to a large category of pictures self-consciously intended to evoke thoughts about death and damnation, life and afterlife, . . . subjects that to us might seem to be far removed from the representation of "mere" flora—not much of that body of meaning attaches to the flowers growing in my garden. (p. 11)

However, having studied tulips, Leppert points out that their multiple meanings become attached to visual culture in his consciousness.

> I cannot look at an old Dutch still life with tulips without remembering what I have now learned. A gap is at least provisionally bridged . . . [and] bridging the gap between "then and now" is not just a matter of sorting out the contents of the past and bringing them forward in time. (p. 11)

It is the connection between then and now that extends and creates greater knowledge.

BACK AND FORTH: JUXTAPOSITIONS OF TIME/SPACE

Visual technologies have, in a sense, democratized the visual arts by presenting a wide variety of visual culture to global audiences and blurring the boundaries of fine arts and popular culture. At the same time, this visual culture colonializes the mind. Through this distribution of visual culture, students' lives are enriched who would not otherwise have an opportunity to see so much, yet, acculturating and stereotypical representations confound the democratic purposes of schooling. As discussed above, this leads us to open up possibilities for discussions of the visual arts as not being inherently good for all people and challenges taken-for-granted art concepts of the past.

One of the ways that contemporary visual culture illustrates these dynamics is through connections and juxtapositions of past, present, and future. Postmodern artists often refer to multiple times and ethnic/geographic/psychological locations in a single image or object illustrating the conceptual, if not literal, flux of time and space.

The Problem with Metaphor

Even art concepts that have traditionally been essential to art curriculum have shifted in their importance as a result of the contemporary directions of the visual arts. For example, teaching students about metaphor has long been considered an important foundation of art education because it is one way to help students understand how people establish meaning in and through the arts. The idea of metaphor (representing one thing as another) though is a relatively closed concept. An understanding of metaphor requires a single group consciousness to have been established so that people who encounter the metaphor will be able to suspend disbelief, access a meaning for both parts of the metaphor, and accept the new relationship established between them (thereby connecting one agreed upon meaning to the other).

However, general knowledge and interpretations of the field of concepts through which meaning is established has grown considerably, as has the diversity of social groups who encounter the same vehicles for symbolic meaning. As a result, people encountering the same visual culture will extend meaning differently and in different directions, making the idea of metaphor difficult to maintain.

For example, representation of women and men of color in U.S. filmmaking has historically been problematic to these groups because filmmakers have largely been white men. The general belief in commonalities among white males (who actually illustrate a range of difference) is represented as opposed to female experience and the experience of men of color and yet accepted as universal experience. This has begun to change in recent decades as the work of new filmmakers is being seen by general public audiences, and given attention in educational settings.

Native American filmmakers, such as videographers George Burdeau and Victor Masayesma, Jr., exemplify artists who represent native experience in a more complex and authentic manner than earlier stereoptypical figures of the old American West. In the work of these artists, we see the connection between sensory qualities and social meaning in the representation of nature as an issue of contention among individuals and social groups, rather than as a mere backdrop to film action (Leuthold, 1998).

The idea that visual culture illustrates the ways in which one thing might be represented by another thing is one of many possible ways of making meaning in and through the visual arts. Even the generic concept of art as metaphor (e.g., this painted image is an apple) is being challenged by artists, such as performance artists, who work to make art a lived experience, rather than a symbol. Figure 3.1 illustrates the ways in which metaphor breaks down and the time of visual culture folds back upon itself. Sherrie Levine's *Fountain (after Marcel Duchamp: A.P.)* refers to Marcel Duchamp's *Fountain*, which was a "ready-made" urinal signed "R. Mutt" and exhibited as a challenge to definitions of art. Levine has pointed to the value that has been placed on Duchamp's work in her bronze recreation of it, which is not so much a metaphor (something as something else) as a dialectic of references each to the other and to ideas outside of the object.

The Visualized Past and Future

The past and the future coexist in the present. Satellite communications and space travel have changed people's conceptions of "home." Science fiction ideas have shaped visual culture, ranging from painting and sculpture to sites on the Internet. Through animatronics, artists who work on feature films combine puppetry, models, and electronics to create science fiction creatures and environments that recycle imagery from the past. In *Jurassic Park III*, animatronics reached a new level of complexity when puppet masters and computer graphic artists worked together to create images of lifelike dinosaurs based on a combination of the newest theories about the creatures and Hollywood-hype style. Some of this imagery references images we have in our heads based on years of viewing artists' and scientists renditions of dinosaurlike creatures, from paintings of St. George and the dragon to *Dinotopia*, the television series with talking dinosaurs. Greek and Roman mythology is recycled in Harry Potter movies and television series like *Xena* and *Hercules*. These visual forms connect with images even young children have seen and will see in the future. For example, I observed a teacher

Figure 3.1. Sherrie Levine, *Fountain (after Marcel Duchamp: A.P.).* 1991. Bronze.

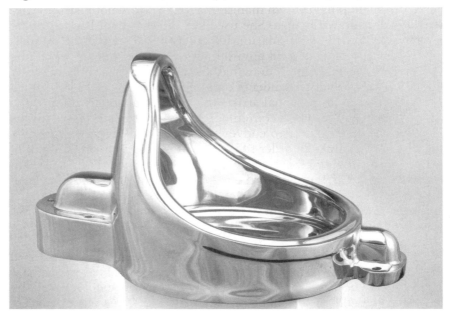

Collection Walker Art Center, Minneapolis. T.B. Walker Acquisition Fund, 1992.

teaching a lesson on mythology to elementary school students who, when she displayed a historical representation of Cerberus, shouted out "Fluffy," the name of the three-headed dog in the first Harry Potter film.

The idea that sci-fi/fantasy is only of interest to a few fans who are geeks or girls interested in more active role models than women in romance fiction has changed. In 1991, the 25th anniversary of the release of the first *Start Trek* series, 53% of all people surveyed said that they were fans of the series. If this was the case (and based on the subsequent success of the series' sequels, that number may now be even greater), the notion of fandom needs to be reconsidered for visual culture (Tulloch & Jenkins, 1995). A great many students are interested in the future. Visual culture sci-fi/fantasy provides an access to visions of possible futures and, as a result, influences their cognitive and aesthetic development.

The popular culture imagery of sci-fi/fantasy is recycled in student art. Some students develop sophisticated worlds of imagery based on this visual culture. I have had the opportunity to experience such rich student investigations through my own students' work and the work of other teachers' students. For example, one high school student focused on developing her own manga imagery. She did not just copy previously adult-drawn manga. She used her International Baccalaureate program to provide a foundation for creating her own, professional-looking fantasy society and environment based on manga style. She works continuously on her drawings and designs, has a website of her work, and talks to other students on-line about it.

Student and professional artists often simultaneously refer to the past, present, and future in contemporary imagery. Historically, artists have used the visual arts to convey multiple meanings, even disguising certain meanings in order to convey messages to a small group of people or to circumvent certain restrictions by authorities. Visual culture apparently directed toward one group may in fact be directed toward another, as in the case of McDonald's or Disney advertisements aimed at children (so that they will convince their parents to buy), but also directed toward adults (through images of well-behaved children and happy families).

Many contemporary artists depend on multiple readings developed through the circumnavigation of time/space, resulting in layered meanings that are accessed as a result of the past experience of viewers who have experienced a wide range of visual culture. They use or suggest bits of our visual and visualized past, recycling ideas and images to jar old memories from our minds and transform them into something new. In the following, I will briefly discuss three artists who use these qualities in their work. These artists are Matthew Barney, Roshini Kempadoo, and Ian Howard.

Matthew Barney. The images Matthew Barney produces are powerful, memorable, and highly suggestive. He produces theatrical, visual narratives. Barney studied art and theater in college and is now a video artist, sculptor, painter, makeup artist, fashion designer, hairdresser, actor, director, and so on. His work can be called fine art because it appears in art museums, but it has also been discussed, for example, in a major fashion magazine.

Barney's work is intellectually challenging, sexually provocative, and may seem even nightmarish (see Figure 3.2). It often focuses on issues of gender and identity in highly imaginative ways. Barney manipulates bodies, sometimes in what seems painful ways, in order to break us out of our ideas of physical limitation. He works with (and against) the human body to create beings that at once reference things we know, things we believe, and things we know cannot be believed. His work involves recycling fantasy beings that exist in our memories based on myths and

Figure 3.2. Matthew Barney, *Cremaster 4*. 1995. Video still.

Collection Walker Art Center, Minneapolis. T.B. Walker Acquisition Fund, 1995.

fairy tales. He creates pastoral characters that reference stories and images from the past and places them in contemporary, often urban, environments. In one video, for example, two centaurs in a limousine fight
as one tries to draw on the window of the limousine. Many of his beings
are neutered through the use of makeup, costumes, and prostheses. Barney
disallows stereotypes by establishing the necessity of multiple layers of
suggestion, not allowing us to settle on any one meaning.

Roshini Kempadoo. The work of artist Roshini Kempadoo is about
issues of race, gender, and beauty in the mass media. The artist places
photographs of herself in layouts that look like fashion magazines, but
are jabs at the ways in which the beauty industry uses women. This
work, like much postmodern fine art, focuses on the relationship be-

tween various forms of visual culture and the place of these forms in a free society. In fact, it cannot be understood without a consideration of that relationship. If members of the audience are familiar with the contexts of being women, "Black," "readers" of fashion magazines, and so on, intended meanings of Kempadoo's work emerge.

Kempadoo's work investigates issues of identity through appropriation of the beauty magazine and other mass media formats through which beauty is defined in Western culture. It raises the issue of "blackness" or "whiteness" as conditions of beauty at the same time as addressing general qualities of being female and living in a society that defines beauty in unrealistic ways. By appropriating the format, and using her own image as the ideal, she makes beauty "real."

Ian Howard. The connections made between the identity of artist and audience, education and entertainment, and art and science are given attention in Australian artist Ian Howard's work. Fantastic images of beings and places and combinations of reality and fantasy are becoming part of the everyday visual world. These border-crossing tendencies are suggested by Ian Howard's work and give it a postmodern flavor.

Graeme Sullivan (1994) has written about Ian Howard in his book *Seeing Australia.* Howard has done appropriations, such as rubbings of military aircraft, and uses recycled toys and other common cultural objects in his work. His art references the influence of the military, concepts of outer space, and science fiction. Sullivan quotes the artist:

> It was a major discovery for me to realise the institutional nature of the link between actual war machines, war toys, and movies about war. They were all part of a military culture saturated with images of war and all accepted as normal. And there was much evidence to be found during my investigations into the military industrial complex in the United States. The classic example of it was in the NASA hangar where they were storing *Enola Gay* [the plane used to bomb Hiroshima] , in the same hangar was the model they used in the *Star Trek* series . . . So, what, in fact, they were doing was entertainment and fantasy with their own military culture that had equal status and equal value. (p. 138)

Sullivan states, "Howard believes that it is crucial for artists to maintain a socially critical stance" (p. 142). As an educator, Howard shaped his curriculum based on the essential relationship between contemporary art and contemporary life and illustrated the importance of cultural response as a didactic, artistic process.

CONCLUSION

In societies that have maintained Euro-American traditions, people have bracketed fine art as something special not only in appearance, but also in academic worth. The study of fine art of the past has been viewed quite differently from the study of other forms of visual culture and the people who make them. However, in contemporary democracies, these conceptual boundaries have been challenged, revealing that an education in visual culture must include an opening up of disciplinary boundaries if we want students to understand ways in which the past lives in the present and future.

New educational representations of the past that infuse ideas and practices involving the social relevance of visual culture are important to making meaning in the postmodern world. Foundations of educational change come from new academic histories of the visual arts, which help to frame discussions of diversity and social meaning, but also come from outside of academic structures to personal stories and visual culture in daily life.

CHAPTER 4

Art and Cognition

Knowing Visual Culture

THE HISTORICAL SEPARATION OF KNOWLEDGE FROM FEELING as a foundation of Western philosophy has devalued the importance of emotion to cognition and resulted in a lack of serious consideration in education of the realm of life called the arts (Eisner, 1998). A body of knowledge has been built on topics related to children's artistic production, particularly the behaviors surrounding drawing development. However, much less attention has been given to the relationship between cognition and the arts. The scientific rhetoric that has shaped educational discourse has guided attention away from the importance of the arts to learning and, for most of the history of public schooling, art has received little attention from those scientists who have been interested in studying what can be easily measured.

Recently, however, cognitive scientists have become interested in the realm of the arts and the relationship of the arts to cognition. This interest stems from the mid-20th century cognitive revolution in psychology and other sciences which reopened the possibility of theorizing about the internal processes that had been ignored by the focus on behaviorism (Anderson, 1980; Baars, 1986). As part of this revolution, sociocultural aspects of cognition have become central to research and theory.

Some of the processes involved in viewing visual culture are psychobiological. For example, human beings only see a narrow band of waves in the electromagnetic spectrum. Everything we see, from a painting in a museum to an ad in a magazine, are perceptible to us because the light that they reflect is in this narrow band. Neon signs, television, computer screens, and kinetic light sculptures emit light in this band. Anything outside this band is imperceptible to the naked human eye.

But the cognitive processing that takes place when we encounter visual culture is a combination of both psychobiological and sociocultural effects. Visual culture engages us on multiple levels with our environment. Although the psychobiological processes that become engaged when we see visual culture may seem mechanistic, we come to know and use our knowledge to engage with our environment in different, individual ways and in ways influenced by social groups. It is a group decision to put ads on television every 10 to 15 minutes, but it is our individual decision to watch them and, if we do, watch them critically. Education and other sociocultural experiences influence our thinking, which becomes transformed into those personal and cultural approaches to the world. For example, the way that we react to color is dependent upon the construction of the human eye and its relation to the brain, but it is also dependent on the social conditions that result in our personal and cultural response based on the relationship between form, feeling, and knowing. This response could be quite different in some Asian countries where red is a symbol of happiness and traditionally used in wedding apparel and other countries where traditional wedding dresses are white and a red dress would be seen as inappropriate.

APPROACHING VISUAL CULTURE: THE RELATIONSHIP OF FORM, FEELING, AND KNOWING TO LEARNING

Our psychobiological responses to visual culture, and some of the reasons for its production, have much to do with the ecology of our development as human beings. In general, we see to recognize, rather than to appreciate, because our most motivating interests have always been to protect ourselves from harm and we must continually be aware of any form that we feel can sustain us or put us in jeopardy, whether it is a wild animal in our cave or a strange car in our driveway. Our first response to visual form in the environment is to determine whether it is familiar (if so, we know what to expect) and whether and how we will engage with it. We tend to look longest at things that are intriguing, but not overwhelming. People are not likely to visually study things that are simplistic or predictable, and when things are chaotic or threatening, we tend to look away. It is between these that the range of our visual attention span functions, but this range tends to change as we develop greater visual experience, individually and as cultural groups, which is why censored imagery of the past that greatly angered some viewers may seem tame to us now.

The Importance of Emotions to Learning:
The Example of Expectation

The relationship between form, feeling, and knowing is an important part of cognitive processing. In regards to visual culture, this relationship involves the processing of contexts as part of the processing of images and objects. Consider the role of expectation in the perception and interpretation of form. Expectation is an emotional state tied to knowledge, often knowledge of form, as in the case of not immediately recognizing someone we know well but do not expect to see in that particular setting.

Great works of art are often considered great because they go beyond expectations. Members of professional arts communities find images and objects that are difficult to understand interesting because they expect to understand art easily; but, at the same time, they hope for a challenge. Art that challenges them to consider their own relationship to it, and promotes a response of intellectual surprise, creates new expectations, illustrating the connection between emotion and cognition. Artist Fred Tomaselli explains this, as quoted in an article in *Artnews* (Sheets, 2000):

> When I first saw a James Turrell piece, I laughed, because I thought it was a stupid modernist dark square painted on the wall of a dimly lit gallery. Then I tried to touch it, my hand went through empty space, Tomaselli recalls, referring to how Turrell manipulates lighting to create illusions of flat shapes. "I went from laughing at it to thinking, 'Ooh.' It challenged what I thought art was. (p. 130)

When viewers do not have a critical understanding of visual culture, looking at, for example, rock videos or minimalist paintings (both of which can be interpreted as having great meaning) can seem a waste of time because they may not be connected to the viewer's previous, complex knowledge. This is an interesting aspect of viewing because people usually think of an image as being safe to look at, even if it is a bit scary, which makes violent images very attractive. However, people who see a work of art that is apparently unrelated to anything they have seen before might respond as if it is threatening. Many adults, including adult students, have negative emotional responses to new visual culture, in part because they tend to have the expectation (interest and emotional investment) that they will generally understand the world. This was the case with three undergraduate students (not majoring in art) that I took to a contemporary art museum early in their course with me. Before entering the museum, I noticed them standing together away from the rest of the students and they did not look well, so I asked them what was wrong. They explained to me that they felt physically ill. In a short conversation, I learned of their symptoms (butterflies in the stomach, dry mouth, and sweaty palms) and that this was their first visit to a contemporary art museum. I explained to the students that these were typical fear symptoms. They were afraid they would fail to understand. But after instruction, when they left the museum, they were happy, excited, and had arranged to visit the museum together again.

Such strong emotions can also result when students who have been previously convinced that they are incapable of making art are asked to do so. These emotions in students become part of their educational history.

> The stories pre-service teachers tell about art—about anger, fear, and jealousy—have become part of their educational history and will certainly influence their future relationship with art, both in and outside of the classroom. Grounded in past events, these stories have taken on the character of mythic accounts for people who are trying to deal with strong feelings that have helped shape their views of life. (Smith-Shank, 1993, p. 46)

⨍ Children are often more accepting of ambiguity in visual culture because they do not have the same feelings tied to understanding. Rather, they have different emotional-cognitive responses, which are also tied to their interests, such as active involvement, that promote learning. Emotion in school subjects other than art is usually considered best left at the classroom door where cognition, without ties to emotion, supposedly takes over. However, learning takes place based on cognitive connections, including those that relate to emotion, and more connections mean greater learning. Learning is dependent on student engagement, which is an indicator of emotional investment.

Cognitive Processing as Making Meaning

When we look at visual culture, our cognitive processing begins with analyses of primitive features—that is, simple forms, in the visual cortex. We first perceive edges and contrasts, shapes and colors. Such raw sensory signals are chaotic, random, and meaningless until they encounter a decoding mechanism, such as the sensory system (the eye) and the corresponding neural system (the brain). The features are quickly analyzed and organized into meaningful relationships, so that we even see lines where they are only suggested and perceive shapes in their simplest form (Arnheim, 1974).

The brain immediately passes these signals on from the eyes to make meaning out of what we see, but meaning may be constructed in many parts of the brain. It takes place not in one location as was thought in the early years of brain research, but in several locations throughout the cerebral cortex simultaneously, and even involves the motor cortex, which stimulates, for example, eye movements:

> At each level the processing becomes more entangled with higher order functions, so that in a very brief time we interpret the visual signals into meaningful thoughts. . . . After the basic perceptual elements of [for example] Degas's romanticized impression are recorded by the eye and optical cortex, the multitude of neural units in the cerebral cortex are compelled to search for "deeper" meaning. (Solso, 1994, p. 30)

Although some specific areas of the brain are mainly responsible for certain brain functions, complex functioning such as viewing a work of art involves the

> simultaneous activation of many areas, a process that has been labeled "massive parallelism." The concept is central to revolutionary new ideas in neurocognition called parallel distributed processing (PDP). This theory posits that the brain functions by distributing impulses throughout large portions of itself in a parallel fashion rather than in a series of steps in which one neuron passes information to another . . . The most important aspect of neural processing is that these multiplicative functions occur in parallel—thus creating a system of analysis that engages countless millions of processing units simultaneously. (Solso, 1994, p. 32–33)

As cognitive psychologist Robert Solso (1994) argues, we are only able to understand the visual arts because of the information we have previously stored about visual features and meanings. When people view a visual array, even our unconscious eye movements are directed by the search for information that will help to make sense of the stimulus based on our previous knowledge (e.g., Nodine, Locher, & Krupinski, 1993; Yarbus, 1967). Greater learning across school subjects may mean greater access to knowledge relevant to a greater range of knowledge about the visual arts stored in more parts of the brain. Cognitive research suggests some of the reasons that it is inappropriate to think of art education from dichotomous perspectives, such as through a focus on form versus meaning or formalism versus contextualism. The more places associations can be established, the more learning takes place.

We learn from artists, including student artists, and their objects. Visual culture includes symbolic forms that make us want to look. Our processes of cognition lead us to want to decipher these forms. Whether the viewing context is considered educational or entertaining, we often approach visual culture as we approach any symbolic form made by other human beings, with an eye toward trying to understand what the artist is trying to "say." We want to decode the artist's intentions, to understand what was in the artist's mind, because we know that visual culture is one of the ways we are connected to our fellow human beings and that its visual character can provide the only access to some aspects of human experience. Our attempts to understand artists' intentions are undertaken, however, at the same time that we construct our own meaning. Through this process, we learn. Because so many environments now depend on this process, we have crossed over the boundaries between education and entertainment, between being students and members of audiences. Through interpretation, the visual arts teach us outside of school and, conversely, in educational settings, they instigate an audience response. Visual culture environments shape artists as they and their objects shape these environments.

Artists often change natural forms to suggest greater meaning, thus defeating our expectations based on previous knowledge. However, in contemporary visual culture, representations shape cognition in ways that collapse the border between reality and representation. Advertisements, films, soap operas, news programs, computer games, and so on, can lead to a cognitive fusion of visual culture and the fiction that is suggested as reality, which depends on and extends the power of the image. Cognition is newly challenged through contemporary visual culture, from the ultra-real 3-D computer animation television cartoon *Max Steel* to the creation of documentary-like photographs of historical events that happened before the invention of the camera. Such visual culture can result in misunderstanding and discomfort at the same time that it can enhance and enrich. This new cognitive condition, which responds to what postmodern theorist Jean Baudrillard termed "hyper-reality," acts beyond the limitations of text-based descriptions of reality to a reconsideration of the whole realm of "empirical" knowledge. In the 21st century, visual fictions are part of reality.

Meaning and Memory

As mentioned above, the meanings of visual culture will be different to a person well educated and greatly experienced in the visual arts than to a naïve viewer. Which of us who are trained in art has not noticed or at least not attended to the message of a painting as we have reflected on the medium, the technical skill used, or the composition of the piece? This is not because we look at the form as pure form, but rather because form itself has a special meaning for us. This is demonstrated by the fact that when we see a form very much like other forms we have seen, it may not demand our attention. It is when we see an unpredicted form that we often focus our attention on it, attaching it to our related knowledge of form, in order to make meaning.

It has been the case for centuries that visual culture has been judged to be good because its form and content work in conjunction so that both are symbolic, as in the suggestion of violence in Picasso's *Guernica*. The form of films based on comic book heroes, such as Dick Tracy, Batman, and Spiderman references the comics through the use of high contrast, bright colors, and exaggerated costume, architecture, and so on. Cindy Sherman's photograph, *Untitled #195*, of herself dressed as a founding father is in a pose we would expect to see in the center of the frame, but she has placed herself off-center, partly outside of the frame, suggesting the postmodern decentering of the heroic male figure. And, in the 11th-century work of the Chinese painter Fan Kuan, *Traveling among the Mountains and Streams*, the scale of nature supports the meaning of the painting and the meaning we bring to the painting gives strength to the form. The meaning we bring to this painting comes from our experiences with nature, information about Chinese culture and painting of the period, other images, and so on. As a result of formal support of narrative suggestion, different knowledge can be accessed simultaneously in the process of making meaning, resulting in more cognitive connections and more knowledge locations to be accessed in the future.

Since the Enlightenment, philosophers have argued that the ways in which we make associations to form new ideas have their origins in sensory experience and reflections on that experience. As discussed in Chapter 2, John Dewey (1934) used experience as the foundation of his approach to art and education. For Dewey, "a work of art . . . is actually, not just potentially, a work of art only when it lives in some individualized experience" (p. 108). In other words, an expressive object, regardless of the meaning of the production for the artist, does not have inherent meaning; the experience of an audience with visual culture makes it meaningful. More recently, cognitive scientists have shown this experimentally and demonstrated the importance of previous knowledge in the construction of knowledge (e.g., Norman, 1993).

Cognitive psychologists call some of the associations that result from the workings of our neural network a "hidden unit." When we see a work of art, regardless of whether it is realistic or nonobjective, we access knowledge stored in our memories. A hidden unit is a concept for which no direct information is given in the work, but we access this concept because the work reminds us of it by extension. Based on these hidden units, we draw narrative and other semantic conclusions about the work and learn as a result of developing these connections (Solso, 1994).

PSYCHOBIOLOGICAL CONCEPTIONS OF ARTISTIC DEVELOPMENT

Conceptions of artistic development have been so influential in art education literature that they may represent the most researched area of the field. This research has primarily focused on drawing development and the notion of an innate process of psychological development that is based on universal stages revealed in children's drawings. This idea emerged with the growth of psychology as a social science near the turn of the 20th century, which provided a basis for research on the influence of innate factors of mental growth. However, as will be discussed below, these early ideas about stagelike development have changed as a result of further research. Twentieth-century accounts of artistic development have largely focused on psychobiological explanations; however sociological considerations are gaining increasing attention (Kindler, 1997; Freedman, 1997a). In the next section, I first discuss two psychobiological conceptions of artistic development, then sociological perspectives.

Stage-by-Age Development

The analysis of children's drawings was an important part of early child study research (e.g., Barnes, 1908; Hall, 1911; Sully, 1895). Child study psychologists supported the conceptualization of children's development in terms of stages of growth that depended on chronological age. This idea led to models that represented children's artistic development as a naturally unfolding, unchangable process that moved toward increasing realism (e.g., Golomb, 1974; Kellogg, 1969; Kershensteiner, 1905, cited in Werckmeister, 1977; Lowenfeld, 1947, 1957; Lowenfeld & Brittain, 1964; Schaefer-Simmern, 1950; Sully, 1895).

Toward the middle of 20th century, experimental psychology increasingly shifted from mental states to limit the study of learning to overt behaviors (Anderson, 1980; Baars, 1986). Because children's drawings could be easily analyzed as behaviors and were a source of data from children who could not yet give effective verbal or written responses, they were considered important to developmental research. The theories of development that resulted from such research were strongly based on the assumption that drawn responses reflected natural characteristics of growth, leading to universal models of development describing sequential, behavioral stages.

The mythology of "the normal child" was extremely important to these models and the research upon which they were based. Although the social and political milieu of the United States directed the new social science of psychology toward questions of children's individual differences, the behaviorism and its related methodologies resulted in analyses of artistic behavior generalized from small, homogeneous groups to large, heterogeneous populations. As a result, the scientific conception of individualism was framed by standards based on group norms. For example, psychologist Edward L. Thorndike (1913) was interested in innate potentials for abnormal and outstanding behavior. His study of *individual* differences involved the collection of data from an array of behavioral tests, including drawing tests, which actually resulted in definitions of innate capabilities in terms of *groups*, such as female and male. Thorndike and other researchers in the early part of the century saw drawing tests as illustrative of various mental capacities and several used children's drawings, particularly of human figures, as measures of intelligence (Cox, 1993).

Researchers allowed group differences to be defined in terms of social value. Psychologists, such as Thorndike, claimed that gender differences in drawings reflected boys' greater intellect. Even into the mid-1900s, researchers such as Gessell (1940) argued that differences between drawings by young boys and girls of the same age indicated that boys were inherently more creative than girls. This was the case even though the differences included such arbitrary defining characteristics of creativity (by the standard of realism, which waned as abstract expressionism became popular) as boys' greater attention to action versus girls' greater attention to detail. However, later research indicated that few formal sex differences exist, and those that do may indicate that girls develop more quickly than boys (see Cox, 1993, for a review). This suggests that differences in form and content between girls' and boys' drawings exist largely because they reflect gender socialization.

From the perspective of these early developmental models, children progress from one stage to the next in a predictably linear process, some moving through the stages more quickly than others, but all moving in the same sequence. The role of art teachers and curriculum has been to aid in that progression by enabling children to move freely through the stages, but in a timely fashion. This perspective of artistic development treats curriculum as a scientific variable that is dependent upon "the normal child's" natural progression. The curriculum implications of stage-by-age development include the idea that certain media production activities should be matched to sequential stage-by-age dependent behaviors.

Expert-Novice Developmental Models

In contrast to the stage-by-age models, expert-novice stage models of development are based on the steps of learning required to advance from a novice level of knowledge to higher-order expertise. This type of stage model has influenced curriculum by shifting the notion of sequentiality from age-dependent levels of "natural" development toward a sequence of levels based on expertise in a discipline. Stage-by-age models involve the assumption that children can innately perform certain behaviors at certain times, whereas expert-novice stage models represent learning in terms of increasingly complex levels of a particular domain of knowledge.

Although authors of both types of models refer to development as dependent to a greater or lesser extent on interaction with the world, these models are fundamentally representations of individually motivated behaviors. However, expert-novice models were conceptualized as part of the cognitive revolution (Baars, 1986). Expert-novice conceptions of development began to be studied seriously in the 1960s with the shift from a focus on traditional behavioralistic research to research concerning complex performances and, by the late 1970s, learning processes (Langley & Simon, 1981). These changes occurred as educational theorists, such as psychologist Jerome Bruner and art educator Manuel Barken, became interested in making education more closely resemble its parent disciplines for social, political, and economic, as well as psychological, reasons. Scientific expert-novice models gained credibility as educators were pressed to create curriculum based on adult domains of knowledge, requiring an understanding of the ways in which proficiency was gained in those domains.

Expert-novice research indicates that age may not be the only, or the most important, determining factor in development. Based on the results of this research, formal knowledge "constrained by principles that govern a domain" (Resnick, 1987, p. 47) is also dependent on the structure of the domain. The research has demonstrated that experts in a field follow different strategies for learning and organizing formal knowledge than do novices (Larkin, 1981). Experts also have multiple levels of knowledge on which they draw when solving problems. However, even adults who have high levels of expertise in the use of traditional art media use processes that reflect novice thinking when learning to use a new medium, such as a computer, to produce art (Freedman & Relan, 1992). This suggests that expertise in the visual arts is tied to situated knowledge as well as knowledge of the structure of a domain.

The research in expert-novice development has involved several disciplines, but has received particular attention in science and math education. The results of this research indicate that theorists should shift from the idea of a global restructuring of knowledge, suggested by a stage-dependent conception of development, to a perspective of learning dependent on the integration of specific concepts (Novak, 1977). Analyses of expert-novice development in art education has been based on research concerning artistic production and response (e.g., Koroscik, 1990; Parsons, 1987).

Unfortunately, when expert-novice approaches that are not based on research (i.e., general conceptions of artist-as-model or classroom-as-studio) have been used in school, much of the complexity of the domains of art has been lost in the application. As a result, two loose translations of art have often been considered curriculum: a rotelike development of production skills and an intuitive leap to a complex level of artistic expression. Harold Rosenberg (1972) termed this reductionism "craft plus inspiration" (p. 47) because, he argued, the most essential aspect of art expertise (that is, the way to get from skill proficiency to the creation of art) was not handled effectively in education.

Both stage-by-age and expert-novice research have provided some information helpful to art education. Stage-by-age models continue to be used in addressing some aspects of development that are important to curriculum planning, particularly at the elementary school level. Expert-novice models have aided researchers and educators to more fully understand the character of learning and applying formal knowledge. Such research concerning the psychological characteristics of artistic development has helped to explain certain psychobiological aspects of growth.

However, attempts to devise both age-by-stage or expert-novice stage models concerning art have had inherent sociological problems on at least four levels. First, behavioral analyses have resulted in classifications of people by groups without consideration of group dynamics. Second, the learning of informal knowledge, an important aspect of knowing visual culture, has not been taken into account. Third, the social attributes of image construction, such as the recycling of imagery, were not given serious attention as part of the learning process (until

Wilson and Wilson began their work in drawing development in the 1970s). Fourth, the social construction of art disciplines was not analyzed to reveal its part in expert-novice development.

The following section focuses on the recent movement toward conceptions of development and learning that increasingly take sociocultural and other situated (contextual) factors into account. Recent research suggests that development is more dependent on teaching and learning than previously thought, which has important implications for curriculum. I will refer to this movement as the sociological approach to the study of development, although it includes research by psychologists, and argue that such considerations should be an important aspect of curriculum (Freedman, 1997a).

SOCIOLOGICAL PERSPECTIVES
OF ARTISTIC DEVELOPMENT

The development of psychology in the United States had strong positivistic foundations that focused studies of learning in individuals as if isolated from social life. This perspective of cognition was helpful for the study of some aspects of learning, but much learning takes place in the context of social conditions that shape what and how people come to know. The study of cognition took a different route in, for example, the Soviet Union, where psychologist Lev Vygotsky based his research on a social conception of development. Differences in ideology and language limited access to this research in North America until after the Cold War, during which U.S. psychologists had spent much of their energy on understanding relationships between human and machine information processing.

As psychologists in the United States increasingly focused attention on the study of cognition, the work of sociologists and anthropologists became understood as more closely associated with the ways in which people's minds worked. Boundaries blurred between these and other social sciences involved with the understanding of learning. A new sociological conception of development emerged as a result of efforts to account for previously ignored sociocultural influences.

Social Learning and Visual Culture

By the 1970s, a more sociological approach to research on children's drawing development was undertaken by art educators Brent Wilson and Marjorie Wilson. The Wilsons formulated a conception of development based on Paget's (1932) suggestion that drawing behaviors reflected social learning. Wilson and Wilson (1977) demonstrated that children learn to draw from many cultural sources, including other children, the mass media, and other adult forms of representation. According to their data, these influences can be seen in structure as well as content.

Wilson and Wilson rejected the notion of drawing schema, which Lowenfeld (1957) described as the symbolic forms children use to represent generic types of objects, such as a person or a tree. For Lowenfeld, schema were stable concepts that do not change form until a child requires another mode of representation, at which time the child develops a new schema through experimentation. Wilson and Wilson (1977) argue that the concept of a drawing program (somewhat like a computer program) is more apt. They postulate that children develop thousands of symbolic programs for objects that may be called upon at any time to represent an object. The programs may be repeated several times and often with certain changes to make a generic form more particular.

This sociological perspective of artistic development takes into account the psychobiological effects that are especially apparent before the increase in social interactions and influences that occur when children enter school. Although children begin their social life at birth, they tend to reflect fewer socializing conditions in their preschool drawings than the drawings they do in kindergarten and later (e.g., Cox, 1993; Gardner, 1991). Once students reach school age, mechanisms from inside and outside the institution work to influence their art. One influence is the school art style of children's art that is only found within the institution and which supports the sociopolitical interests of public school socialization (Efland, 1976).

Although the purposes of public school art education have sociocultural roots, children have been represented in curriculum as though they are without attributes of culture. Such a conception of individualism supports the idea of a fictional free self-expression in school (an inherently social institution) through the teaching of art (a product of cultural communities). The focus on this conception of "natural" individualism in curriculum has resulted in the neglect of both cultural similarities and differences. The sociocultural attributes that confound this notion of individualism, such as the influence of schooling, mass media, and gendered/ethnic experience, have received little attention by researchers in art education (Freedman, 1994).

Researchers who have studied the sociological aspects of artistic development argue that several aspects of drawing are connected to a wide range of cultural influences. Universal schema are questioned in the light of evidence from increasingly diverse school populations. Researchers have demonstrated that forms of children's drawing development are not universal (e.g., Brittain, 1990; Kindler, 1994; see also Cox, 1993, for a review). The contents and structures of children's drawings differ across histories and cultures, indicating that development is influenced by time and place. Contemporary conceptions of artistic development must include a consideration of the influence of postmodern visual culture on students. Rather than being a linear progression to a prespecified endpoint, development is the construction of repertoires of expression that cross symbol systems (Kindler, 1999).

In the postmodern world, student artistic production and response reflects the environment of mass-produced and distributed visual culture. Children create whole worlds through the development of figures based on, for example, computer games, manga, and music videos. The influence of visual culture is seen at more mature levels of development, too, such as exhibitions of university student computer art in which many of the images look like the fictional landscapes seen in sophisticated computer games like Myst and Riven.

Learning as Restructuring Knowledge: The Infusion of Interpretation and Critical Reflection

As suggested above, cognitive theory researchers generally agree on the importance of prior knowledge in learning (e.g., Joyce & Weil, 1986; Marzano, 1992), and specifically, "most of the learning that occurs in life is either incorporated within prior knowledge (Piaget's *assimilation*) or modifies prior knowledge (Piaget's *accommodation*)" (Vosniadou & Brewer, 1987, p. 51, italics in original). Students learn by restructuring information they encounter in relation to their previous knowledge (Vosniadou & Brewer, 1987). Such restructuring influences the processes used to learn further information. If the information encountered is consistent with previous knowledge, it will be assimilated; if it is inconsistent, it may be rejected or changed to fit what is already known. At times, this restructures new knowledge to fit with old results in misinterpretations. They may inappropriately restructure old knowledge when faced with inconsistent new information if they have not been taught to approach such information as a positive challenge (Prawat, 1989). Simple information is easiest to assimilate or reject and highly complex new information is likely to be rejected (Vosniadou & Brewer, 1987).

As a result, students should come to understand that, from an educational perspective, interpretation must include critical reflection. The infusion of critical analysis and interpretation when making and viewing visual culture leads to learning conceived as a highly interactive process. At the same time as students develop ideas, attitudes, and beliefs in and through visual culture, they should be reflecting on that development and the way in which it changes them as they learn.

Although subtle changes in knowledge occur on a continual basis, radical restructuring of knowledge seems to emerge with age or expertise. This periodic restructuring of knowledge, considered by Piaget and others to be a global developmental change, involves interaction with the world. Researchers are in debate about whether a global approach to learning, such as Piaget's, should be replaced by one that is more domain-specific, in part to explain developmental differences between novices and experts.

However, an interpretation of development that takes into account increasingly complex social conditions, including our encounters with visual culture, is likely to require a new definition of knowledge and knowing that will include moving beyond Piaget's conception of formal thinking. From this perspective formal thinking in the Piagetian sense involves

> an acceptance of a mechanistic worldview that is caught in a cause-effect, hypothetico-deductive system of reasoning . . . formal, operational thinkers accept an objectified, unpoliticized way of knowing that breaks a social or educational system into its basic parts in order to understand how it works. Emphasizing certainty and prediction, formal thinking organizes verified facts into a theory. The facts that do not fit the theory are eliminated, and the theory developed is the one best suited to limit the contradictions in knowledge. (Kincheloe & Steinberg, 1993, p. 297)

Kincheloe and Steinberg (1993) argue that a postformal model of thinking is necessary given recent illuminations of social influence on thought by social scientists and researchers in the humanities. They suggest that researchers interested in children's development should focus on social conditions surrounding the construction of knowledge, such as underlying assumptions of knowledge, processes of thought and knowing, and contextual relationships in order to better understand the complex way that learning occurs. Each of these involves emotional states and social conditions, such as the ways in which students make and view visual culture, and includes interactions with various forms that suggest meaning. This is illustrated by the example of artist Jenny Holzer's stone bench work in Figure 4.1, which includes text through which meaning may be established based on personal experiences; but is also a comment on social interactions and references more general social meanings, including those related to encountering art in a museum.

Figure 4.1. Jenny Holzer, *It Takes a While.* 1993. Granite.

IT TAKES A WHILE BEFORE YOU CAN
STEP OVER INERT BODIES AND GO AHEAD
WITH WHAT YOU WERE TRYING TO DO

Collection Walker Art Center, Minneapolis. Anonymous gift from a local resident with appreciation for the Minneapolis Sculpture Garden and contemporary art, 1993.

SOCIAL WAYS OF KNOWING ART:
CONSTRUCTIVISM, SOCIALLY SHARED
COGNITION, AND DISTRIBUTED COGNITION

The idea of knowledge as socially constructed led to the study of socially shared cognition. Socially shared cognition is at the root of learning communities, which are a foundation for teachers and students
acting in groups. The concept of learning communities has many
sources, not the least of which are cultural and professional communities that promote certain ways of thinking and recognize agreed-upon
realms of knowledge and assessment. A look at the history of these ideas
will help to explain their application.

Sociohistorical Psychology

Although the first U.S. translation of Lev Vygotsky's work appeared in
1962, little attention was given to it until the 1980s. Vygotsky's milieu
enabled an acceptance of the sociohistorical character of knowledge as
inherent in cognitive research. Unfortunately, at the time in the United
States, psychology was defined by positivism and behaviorism, which
not only showed little concern for mental processes, but also did not
take into consideration the social dialectic of learning.

Shifts in the study of learning and human development toward
social questions have resulted in new ways to think about individual
cognition enabling Vygotsky's work to gain increasing influence in the
United States. Vygotsky's work focused on, among other things, the
impact of the cultural settings in which a student learns. He argued that
learning not only *occurs in* context, but is *driven by* context. Sponta-
neously learned concepts are heavily dependent on individual drive, but
systematic concepts, such as (professional) scientific concepts, shape
how students learn as well as what they learn.

Vygotsky's discussion of scientific concepts can be related to the
ways in which students learn about artistic concepts. Professional art
communities influence what is taught about art in the cultural setting of school and how it is taught. As mentioned above, arts communities are redefining art concepts to focus to a greater extent on social
context.

Constructivism: Socially Constructed Knowledge

The general sociological direction taken by many developmental researchers is reflected in constructivist learning theory. Constructivist

learning theory is based on some aspects of Piaget's early work, but more recent research has expanded on his early vision. This research has suggested that all learning is situated or closely related to the circumstance in which it takes place (e.g., Resnick, 1987; Walkerdine, 1988). From this perspective, development is bound by students' construction of knowledge rather than the other way around.

Constructivism is, in a sense, a poststructural theory of cognition in that it moves away from immutable, universal structures (Doll, 1993). It has roots in Dewey's pragmatism, and constructivist concepts of learning were introduced in the work of Piaget in the 1930s. Knowledge cannot represent some independent reality; rather, the mind creates knowledge in order to adapt to reality. Although some philosophers and cognitive scientists continue to argue that independent representations of reality and intelligence exist, many contemporary educators and cognitive scientists have agreed with evidence that the mind creates knowledge in response to the world, as it creates and recreates itself.

Learning occurs through the social mediation of an interdependent world of knowledge (Lave, 1991). The mediation takes place in a social community as a result of historical traditions that are renewed and changed during mediation. The problem for educators is to develop an approach to teaching that can aid students in analyzing the mediation as it occurs. This approach needs to take into account five general principles of constructivist conceptions of learning (Fosnot, 1996):

1. Learning is not the result of development; learning *is* development.
2. Disequilibrium facilitates learning.
3. Reflective abstraction is the driving force of learning.
4. Dialogue within a community engenders further thinking.
5. Learning proceeds toward the development of structures. (pp. 29–30)

Individuals are part of their sociocultural milieu. A lack of attention to this condition has masked aspects of development situated in and not independent of contextual environment (Cole & Engestrom, 1993). This environment includes the social setting of a classroom. In a study of individual contributions of students to shared knowledge, Brownell and Carriger (1991) found that students shape contexts as contexts shape them. It is a highly interactive relationship, dependent on communication, that requires common ground to be established for communication to occur (Krauss & Fussell, 1991). Such communication necessitates a teaching approach that is provocative and enables students to make social connections (Prawat, 1996).

The social characteristics of development and intelligence have become a part of the modern versus postmodern debate in education. Kincheloe and Steinberg (1993) reflect this in their discussion of postformal thinking as "grounded in an understanding of critical and postmodern advances in social theory" (p. 296).

> One of the main features of post-formal thinking is that it expands the boundaries of what can be labeled as sophisticated thinking . . . The modernist conception of intelligence is thought of as an exclusionary system . . . [from this perspective] intelligence and creativity are thought of as fixed and innate . . . Indeed, the child in the developmentalist discourse is often viewed, within an ethic of Lockean individualism, as an isolated entity . . . Post-formal thinking attempts to conceive cognition in a manner that transcends the essentialist and reductionist tendencies within developmentalism, coupling an appreciation of the complexity of self-production and the role of power with some ideas about what it means to cross borders of modernist thinking. (pp. 298–300)

Kincheloe and Steinberg (1993) address several issues of postmodern education that can aid in the development of postformal thinking. These include the importance of understanding the social origins of knowledge, influences of pattern (underlying social structures, assumptions, and relationships), the power of process (deconstructing social "texts" and connecting logic and emotion), and the necessity for contextualization (giving attention to social settings).

In the contemporary postindustrial world, people have a "bigger picture" of themselves than in the past, a picture that even includes the possibility of beings on other planets, in other galaxies. This group conception of the self in relation to nature, fellow beings, and even the universe is one example of the social dialectic of knowledge working back on itself in ways that make other social knowledge possible. The conception is only possible because of the visual arts and other forms of representation. It is the visualization of other worlds that make such possibilities accessible and believable.

Our representations, and our ability to reflect on them, are the things that make us human. They distinguish us from other species and connect us to other humans. The representations themselves are, in a sense, the milieu in which we develop, and come to know that we are developing.

Distributed Cognition

Until recently, cognitive scientists have focused their research and theory on a conception of pure intelligence, as if it were independent of the social and physical world (Norman, 1993). As discussed above, this conception of learning has appeared to focus on individuals but has actually been about certain social groups, such as groups determined by sex, age, and ethnicity. Out of necessity, researchers have often studied undergraduate psychology students or other groups that were easily accessible, while assuming to be studying individual differences and universal attributes. However, the groups studied by psychologists in research about learning have typically not been studied in the process of social interactions, nor have the artificial characteristics of experimental methodologies been taken into account, and so the argument supporting the idea of pure reason has been maintained.

Recent cognitive science research has become more interdisciplinary, as has the development of "smart machines." A close relationship has existed between conceptions of human cognition and computer information processing since computers were invented. However, as more is discovered about the manner in which we construct knowledge, the metaphors researchers have used to describe the ways in which we come to know have become more concerned with interactions between humans and objects. For example,

> The classroom is, in effect, a "PDP" system (it does Parallel Distributed Processing). [A] class-decision is due to the *parallel processing* (all children chatter simultaneously) of *localized computation* (each child speaks to, and is directly influenced by, only her immediate neighbors), and is *distributed* across the whole community (as an internally consistent set of mini-decision made by all the children). (Boden, 1992, p. 121, emphasis in original)

Artificial experimentation actually may make the tasks that researchers want to study more difficult than they are in daily life because our interactions with everyday objects so heavily influence our cognitive processes (Norman, 1993).

> With the disembodied intellect, isolated from the world, intelligent behavior requires a tremendous amount of knowledge, lots of deep planning and decision making, and efficient memory storage and retrieval. When the intellect is tightly coupled to the world decision making and action can take place within the context established by the physical environment, where the structures can often act as a distributed intelli-

gence, taking some of the memory and computational burden off the human. (p. 147)

Distributed cognition is the understanding that in the real world, objects and people are part of not only what we know, but how we know. Information in the world is a "storehouse of data" (p. 147), and we use the world to help recollect what we need to live, to remind us of things that we must do, and so on. How do we know when it's time to buy groceries? We see an empty container, cabinet, or refrigerator or someone we live with says, "we're low on milk."

Distributed cognition can also be demonstrated through our interactions with the visual arts. Every day we encounter designed objects and images (like containers, cabinets, and other household goods) that are a part of our visual culture environment. We come to a basic understanding of the visual arts through our interactions with visual culture, which are so common in daily life that we sometimes do not notice them. These daily interactions involve learning through images and objects that represent knowledge and mediate relationships between creators and viewers.

SITUATED KNOWLEDGE:
DEVELOPING CONCEPTIONS
AND MISCONCEPTIONS ABOUT ART

Knowledge is constructed in the context of a learning situation. This may occur inside or outside of a classroom. When students learn outside of a classroom, they often learn misconceptions about art or mottoes that may have little meaning for them from an adult perspective, but which may actually have great currency because students use them to demonstrate some knowledge. For example, when a student says that art is "free self-expression," the student has not necessarily reflected on the complex relationship of individual freedom to sociocultural norms that influence choices related to stylistic conventions, subject matter, and so on. So, adults may not know what knowledge the student has actually constructed attached to the phrase except that it is one which has currency in certain settings. Similarly, adolescents often test the meanings of freedom in a democracy when they say to adults, "it's a free country" when they want to do something that breaks the rules.

Smith-Shank (1995) points out that the situated character of learning is important to artistic production and analysis because signs in the

environment interact with and shape student learning. In art classrooms, aspects of the setting are interpreted by students based on their
previous knowledge of art, classrooms in general, school, and so on.
However, these interpretations will also depend on the individual
teacher. Teachers organize and manage classrooms in ways that teach
students, sometimes as part of the hidden curriculum. Students may
interact with and interpret art classrooms as places of work or of play,
as technical studios or studios in which serious and thoughtful study
takes place, or in other ways that become part of student knowledge
about art and art education.

In part, because they learn so much about the arts in informal settings, students of all ages have misconceptions about the arts (e.g.,
Erickson, 1994; Gardner, Winner, & Kirchner, 1975; Parsons, 1987). As
demonstrated by studies of science education, students most often ad-
just new information, even empirical evidence, to fit their previous
conceptions (Champagne, Klopfer, & Anderson, 1980; Joshua & Dupin,
1987). These conditions have led cognitive scientist Lauren Resnick
(1994) to argue that educators need to take at least two different approaches to learning. The first is a response to the learning of "concepts
that are coherent with biologically prepared structures" (p. 489). As
Arnheim (1974) demonstrated about the visual arts through gestalt psychology, humans perceive certain things consistently across individuals as a result of the way we are "wired." The second type of conceptual
development involves learning that is inconsistent with biologically
based structures, based on culturally formed concepts. In the first case,

> it is reasonable to conclude that children's own cognitive constructions
> will move without much resistance toward the cultural[ly] accepted forms
> to which they are exposed. In the case of cultural knowledge that contra-
> dicts biologically preferred concepts, however, education must follow a
> different path: still constructivist in the sense that simple telling will not
> work, but much less dependent on untutored discovery and exploration.
> For these contradictory concepts, ways of helping children replace rather
> than elaborate on initial beliefs need to be found. (p. 489)

Concepts associated with the visual arts are of both types, but those
that are associated with cultural knowledge are the most difficult to
teach. For example, learning to draw well enough to symbolically represent is consistent with basic biological structures. However, learning
to draw using a Western, fine art perspective may not be and therefore
requires a different sort of guidance than does simple symbol making.
Resnick (1994) suggests two ways of going about this in science education, both of which already have currency in art education. The first

involves teaching students core concepts and then guiding them through the application of these concepts in diverse situations. In art, the use of perspective in drawing might be considered one basic concept that can be applied in many different situations. In the second, students apply the concepts mechanically and then develop an understanding and appreciation of them through the success of their application.

CONCLUSION

Coming to know visual culture occurs through the cognitive processes of production and viewing. Teaching visual culture is not just a matter of selecting the images and objects to include in curriculum. It involves changes in the instructional methods used to enact curriculum, changes that should respond to the new understanding of cognition as well as traditional methods that have been demonstrated to work, which will be discussed in the following chapters. These methods should take into account the variety of experiences people have with visual culture and how those experiences direct learning.

CHAPTER 5

Interpreting Visual Culture

Constructing Concepts for Curriculum

WE LIVE IN A WORLD INCREASINGLY SATURATED BY VISUAL culture that influences students at all educational levels. Even newborn babies are given exciting, brightly colored toys that activate still-developing neurons. Advertising photography, bodily fluids, and objects created to be part of the fabric of native, tribal life are all displayed in art museums—but a person does not have to visit an art museum to see forms of visual culture. Each time we watch a television, walk in a mall, sit on a piece of furniture, visit an amusement park, or surf the net, we experience visual forms of representation. The range of places that we see art has expanded to include television, banks, newspapers, shopping malls, parks, and websites. Through mixes of popular visual culture and fine art, new images are produced and new meanings of art (as a category) are learned (Freedman, 1997b). In the process of viewing, people develop ideas about art, ranging from definitions and arts categories to aesthetic judgments and what it means to be "cultured."

For this reason, art is purchased by corporations, not only as a financial investment, but also to legitimize their industry and represent their work as part of high culture and achievement. Because the art is purchased to influence people's thinking about the business, it is not kept in a vault; it is displayed, often in special gallery spaces in the workplace. Displaying the collection in this context focuses signification. The individual works of art are not the only signs in this context. The gallery and collection become signs pointing out that the purposes of industry are the purposes of art; that is, the enrichment of life. In the process, corporate concepts become attached to art, not only to a particular painting or sculpture, but to art as a concept. As a result, cognition takes a somewhat different path than it does when art is housed in a museum. New contexts cause new meanings to be constructed.

In the past, type of media, level of technical skill, and compositional sophistication played a large part in determining whether an object was considered to be a work of art. However, such qualitative differences between visual forms have become less discrete. A heap of garbage arranged by an artist in a museum can be considered a work of fine art and garbage that is part of the visual culture of the environment can be conceptualized as an important visual reflection of human intention. The skills required to produce, analyze, and assess this expanding realm of visual culture are complex, crossing many types of old boundaries, and indicate that a broadening of curriculum is essential. Curriculum must now address objects that are made, seen, and judged in terms of an array of sociocultural positions, interactions, and institutions.

INTERPRETATION, CONTEXTS, AND EXTENDED MEANINGS

Many of the issues that are seen as important in postmodern art and education have existed historically in other forms. However, the new technological presence of visual images and objects, the ease and speed with which they can be produced, and the power of their pervasiveness demands changes in curriculum. In the new visual culture environment, high-level, interdisciplinary interpretive skills and concepts are becoming increasingly important for all students.

Interpretation is the process of giving meaning to form. As discussed in Chapter 4, interpretation is best infused with critical thinking when learning takes place. In order to help students to critically reflect on their interpretations, inquiry should be promoted by teachers and students. Various works of art often require different questions to be asked of them. For example, it may be less appropriate to ask formalistic questions of work done by a postmodern artist than it would be of a De Stijl artist's work. However, if interpretation is understood as a type of inquiry, many different kinds of questions may be asked that open up several possibilities for being "right." Interpretation may not be conceptualized by students as safe because, from an educational standpoint, it must be supportable; but when conceptualized as a type of inquiry, it is also debatable.

Lower-level interpretive skills include the discernment of a simple, intended message of a symbolic representation or personalizing a situation that one sees represented. Higher-level interpretive skills include:

(1) unpacking underlying assumptions, (2) forming multiple, possible associations; and (3) performing self-conscious, critical reflection. Each of these is discussed in the following three sections.

Unpacking Underlying Assumptions: Representing Contexts as a Part of Visual Culture

As discussed in Chapter 3, curriculum should include both contexts of production and viewing, such as cultures, countries, communities, institutions (including schools), and the sociopolitical conditions under which art is made, seen, and studied. Contexts reveal the underlying assumptions with which visual culture is created and seen. In order to understand visual culture and maintain the integrity of the artist and the culture in which it was created, the context of production must be taken into account.

For example, a popular art movement developed in Shaba, Zaire, that can only be understood through the study of the artists' context (Brett, 1987). These artists create at least three different types of paintings: Things Ancestral, Things Present, and Things Past (Szombati-Fabian & Fabian, 1976). Paintings of Things Ancestral are about early tribal life and customs, including romanticized images of daily activities, such as hunting. Things Present focus on contemporary urban industrial life, such as the copper smelting industry. Paintings of Things Past represent historical themes from the time following contact of the Shaba people with outsiders. This type of painting may include images of Arab slave traders and Belgian colonialism. Without information about these contexts, the important difference between these types of painting cannot be understood by students. Unfortunately, the art of tribal cultures is sometimes ridiculed and judged as simplistic by adolescent students when analyzed using the formalistic approach prevalent in U.S. public schools. These students are at a time in their life when representationality of form heavily influences their judgments of artistic quality. However, the same students could be intrigued by this art when considered in relation to issues of identity and the iconographic context in which it was produced.

Contexts also include the interdisciplinary conditions and environments that make student art possible, from what students see every day to sources of their emotions, opinions, and beliefs. They include the underlying interests of adult producers referenced in student art and the theories upon which we base production and viewing education, such as the models of aesthetics, childhood, and curriculum that shape our views about teaching.

Derrida (1976) has taught us that not only multiple, but conflicting meanings are inherently suggested by representation. Often, it is these conflicts that underlie assumptions in visual culture. All sorts of cultural dichotomies—establishment versus antiestablishment, male versus female, nature versus culture—are suggested by visual culture (de Lauretis, 1987). Border conflicts, particularly conflicts at the borders of cultural difference, are often at the center of contemporary visual culture in ways that range from the cross-cultural appropriation of symbols to the colonizing imagery of global technologies. The dichotomization of borders implies that half of each is good and half is bad. It is not surprising, then, that the many meanings of visual culture often seem to confound one another. Oppositional ideas about fine art, such as pleasure versus pain, important versus trivial, freedom versus control, and individual versus society, illustrate underlying assumptions about the subcultural in relation to the fine art community. Border conflicts are established between visual cultural forms, such as popular culture versus fine art, and within forms as well.

To teach visual culture requires interdisciplinary investigations of the underlying assumptions that can be revealed in the conceptual space between images and objects. Consider the example of a television commercial that uses fine art as a way to promote desire for things associated with wealth and power, which is intended to be cultivated and transformed into desire to buy the product. This process is to occur through the juxtaposition of signs that the advertisers assume have been previously defined for their audience, causing intended associations. A voice-over does not have to state, "buy this," or "if you buy this, you will be happier." Simply juxtaposing a product with fine art suggests a metaphorical transformation. Notions of a consumer with good taste, high standards, and refined sensibilities are intended to become attached to the product. The creators of these commercials assume that most of their viewers, adolescents and adults who are part of mainstream American culture, will understand their intent. The targeted audience is thought to associate an appreciation of fine art with being cultured or enlightened. These advertisements work to construct their audience in order to create desire (e.g., Ewen, 1988; Goffman, 1979; Williamson, 1978).

Advertisers know that techniques of juxtaposing and associating a product with fine art influence people's perceptions of the product. However, the reverse happens as well; the techniques influence people's perception of art; art becomes a commodity. Contextual connections may be investigated between and among other visual culture forms as well. For example, relevant discussions of the sexual orientation of heterosexual male fine artists who have focused their work on the creation of idealized and objectified female nudes and that of artists such as Keith Haring and Gilbert and George, who address issues of homosexuality, can be considered along side of body and health images that are common in many forms of visual culture.

As discussed in Chapter 3, the difference between production and viewing contexts is critical and can influence student learning. The arts of traditional cultures are recontextualized when viewed in contemporary contexts. And yet, differences between contexts of making and seeing have not generally been given attention in curriculum. Images are now often seen without the context of their original intent and juxtaposed with previously unrelated imagery that provoke associations created by this new context. The various modes of reproduction that enable viewing on a large scale are productive in the sense that they involve the creation of a new object each time an object is reproduced. The contexts of museums, television programs, advertisements, as well as school curriculum, all influence the ways in which a single work of fine art (and through the exemplar, fine art as a concept) is understood.

Forming Associations: Suggestiveness and the Construction of Multiple Meanings

One of the keys to teaching visual culture is an understanding of the notion of *suggestiveness*. Suggestiveness refers to the associative power of visual culture to lead to emotional, cognitive responses and interactive, multileveled meanings. Viewers turn suggestion into meaning. Suggestiveness promotes extended knowledge to be constructed, making connections between a range of prior knowledge from outside the work.

Several educational models (Broudy, 1972; Feldman, 1967, 1970) of responding to art have emerged in the past that have ignored the importance of suggestiveness to the construction of extended knowledge. Broudy's aesthetic scanning model focused attention on the sensory, formal, media, and expressive aspects (in that order) of the work. Feldman's model is based on the steps description, formal analysis, interpretation, and judgment as a way of postponing judgment until the work has been studied. Both are easily assimilated into curriculum and have helped teachers begin to address the problem of teaching students ways of talking about works of art. However, both of these models require analysis to begin with the object, place undue emphasis on formal and technical attributes of art objects and, perhaps even more important, indicate that interpretations of works of art are only dependent on what is inside the physical borders of the work.

As well as its surface form and content, visual culture is about the people who create it, view it, show it, buy it, study it, and criticize it. This is important to remember if we are to use the little time we have with students to teach them what is most important about visual culture. As a result, art educators such as Tom Anderson (1988; 1993) have refocused models of analysis for use in the classroom to take context into account by, for example, privileging students' personal responses to art and giving attention to knowledge that crosses the boundaries of arts disciplines.

Figure 5.1 illustrates a conceptual framework that infuses considerations of contexts in analyses of artifacts, forms, and experiences.

Critical Reflection: Self-Conscious Awareness of Associative Knowledge

Educators would be delighted if our labor would result in all of the visual arts being interpreted through processes of thoughtful analysis and critique. In order for this to happen, the visual arts and arts communities need to be understood as open systems in which professional and lay people can take part and contribute. The contribution of student interpretation to classroom discussion can be increasingly meaningful as they change their thinking through processes of critical reflection.

As illustrated by the resurgence of figurative work in fine art at the end of the 20th century, postmodern issues of self have shifted from the accumulation of an objectively conceived knowledge to the ways in which knowledge is constructed and used to shape identity. Understanding is as much about who you are as about what you know; it is as much ontological as epistemological. The question of *what we know* has been displaced by the question of *who we are* as the truth "out there" becomes increasingly evasive and seems to collapse back to the one form in which we have confidence: our bodies. The expanding realm of visual culture is not just worthy of study because *it's out there;* it is worthy of study because *it's in here;* through art making and viewing, we shape our thinking about the world and about ourselves.

Giving serious attention to this epistemological instability contrasts with instructional models such as Feldman's (1970), which carry with them the assumption that the information one needs to know in order to interpret a work of art is contained within the work. Feldman maintains that the best interpretation of art is that which uses the most evidence from the work and is a pseudoscientific investigation that

Figure 5.1. A framework for teaching visual culture.

1. PRODUCTION CONTEXTS

    Experience and study the context of production, including cultural purposes of
    production, visual traditions, artists' personal histories, ethnic backgrounds,
    artistic intent, use of mass media images, etc. Context includes historical,
    cultural, political, social, economic, religious, etc. conditions that influenced
    visual production.

2. EXPLORATION CONTEXTS

    Experience and study viewing circumstances, including institutional settings,
    viewer past experience and prior knowledge, image recycling, influences of
    culture and tradition on appreciation, etc. Study includes cultural and personal
    influences on appreciation, such as politics, education, institutional conditions,
    family, mass media, etc.

3. FUNCTION AND MEANING

    Study and articulate multiple perspectives of visual culture(s), including the
    meaning as interpreted by people in the context of production, student
    interpretations, and symbolic, metaphoric and other culturally based qualities of
    interpretation that convey meaning in the context of appreciation. Study
    includes developing an understanding of consensus building and the acceptance
    of conflict in interpretation.

4. STRUCTURAL SUPPORT

    Study and use elements and principles, technical skills required for production
    and use (including appreciation), and various media in creating and analyzing
    visual culture in relation to cultural contexts.

implies the achievement of a preconceived, best outcome. In contrast,
the intended interpretation of much postmodern visual culture may be
no more legitimate than the interpretation based on viewers' associations. From this perspective, a "better" interpretation may be one that
involves more complex, and perhaps unintended, associations. For an
interpretation to be supportable, it will probably reference the work,
but may draw more on, for example, the memory of a personal experience than the work itself. More interpretations mean a more creative
response.

Research has suggested that students and lay adults tend to locate
themselves in the fictional realities of artistic forms (e.g., Beach & Freedman, 1992; Radway, 1985). In one study, high school students did not
tend to view visual and textual fictional sources of stereotypes critically unless they were specifically taught how to do so either formally

in school or by parents or siblings (Beach & Freedman, 1992). Such research suggests that students' encounters with multiple, even fictional realities, are transformed into knowledge. In this study, the students saw the visual fiction of advertising as reality and compared their lived reality unfavorably to the world they created out of visual culture.

High school students rarely make qualitative distinctions between types of imagery (Freedman & Wood, 1999). They tend to respond to images on a level of recognition (not analysis), unless specifically taught how to analyze imagery to decode deeper intended meanings. Nevertheless, students continually create personal and cultural meaning from visual culture which reflects knowledge, beliefs, and attitudes stimulated by an overlapping array of images they have seen in the past (e.g., Beach & Freedman, 1992; Freedman & Wood, 1999). They cross-reference other images and other forms of culture in the process of making meaning.

When students analyze imagery and make thoughtful critical assessments, the assessments tend not to cross visual and textual modes (Beach & Freedman, 1992). Students who have been taught how to critically analyze written texts cannot be assumed to transfer those skills when viewing images. The limited amount of transfer apparent when students are taught primarily in one mode, usually language, is an essential reason for art education. Students with an adequate general education, but little art education, have greater difficulties understanding and interpreting the complex meanings associated with visual cultural forms than do students with a background in the visual arts. Research indicates that even if students receive an art education, but focus only on production skills, they will not be able to successfully analyze historical works of art (e.g., Erickson, 1998; Short, 1998).

An interpretive skill that can help students to critically reflect is the ability to become conscious of associations and connections they develop that go into building their knowledge and judgments. In order to help students to build their knowledge, broadening, rather than narrowing interpretation is critical. Rather than seeking the best, expert interpretation of a work of art, students can broaden their understanding of interpretation and their interpretive skills by finding their own personal and cultural meanings, comparing, combining, and challenging these with the interpretations of others to increase associations and build complexity. Focusing their attention on reflective speaking and writing (in responding to imagery of their choice, in journals, etc.) and introspection illustrated by their own art can help students attend to the reasons for their interpretations. In order to promote the development of interpretive skills and the knowledge-building connections that come with them, students must have opportunities to come to understand the multiple ways in which representation works in visual culture, how it is used, and how to form visual interpretations of their own ideas.

POSTMODERN CONCEPTS AND VISUAL CULTURE

The integral connection between meaning and what has traditionally been conceptualized as (mainstream, analytical) aesthetics can be seen in the increasing impact of imagery over text in mass communications. Artistic production media have always been used by artists to promote certain values, but visual technologies are used in ways that more literally represent and can subtly misrepresent. For example, manipulated photography has become the norm in advertising, and because this form of imagery is so convincing, the manipulations are highly believable. The technological capabilities that have made possible the distribution of art on a global scale have also transformed art into a mass form of culture.

The impact of contemporary imagery has generated a wide range of sociopolitical and economic issues, including its influence on student identity, notions of citizenship, beliefs about democracy, and so on. Consider the Calvin Klien ads for the fragrance Be, where skin blemishes and moles of the model have been shown in order to surprise and draw the attention of an audience expecting to see the hyperreality of computer-manipulated beauty. The surface of the ad tells each viewer to "be yourself"—a critical concept to sales in democratic societies—that is, be a natural individual while convincing us that we should be like the other people who buy the (unnatural) product. The deeper message concerning the conflict inherent to these opposing ideas is complex—and it is the complexity that is attractive. As with sex and death, which are used to sell, we are at once interested in and afraid of the profound implications of freedom.

In order to teach about the complexities of postmodern visual culture, concepts given attention in and around visual culture can be of help. Figure 5.2 presents a list of those concepts.

Text, Imagery, and "Image"

Semiotic theory has been used to suggest that visual images are read as texts. Images are similar to texts in some technical ways. Both images and texts are forms of representation. They depend on the use of meta-

Figure 5.2. Concepts to assist understanding of postmodern visual culture.

1. ART AS CULTURAL PRODUCTION
   a reflection of cultural conditions
   cultural critique
   cultural symbols
   challenges elitism of high modernism

2. TEMPORAL AND SPATIAL FLUX
   environmentalism
   pastiche
   eclecticism
   recycling and transforming

3. DEMOCRATIZATION AND A CONCERN FOR OTHERNESS
   power/knowledge
   pluralism
   popular culture
   less emphasis on "good" aesthetics or "good" design

4. ACCEPTANCE OF CONCEPTUAL CONFLICT
   fragmentation
   dissonant beauty
   collage
   deconstruction

5. MULTIPLE READINGS
   reading images
   issues of representation
   attached meanings
   double-coding

phor and other types of symbolism. They involve recycling and are at times made of the same medium, such as film, television, and even paint. But, the important similarity between images and texts in relation to education is a general one: we construct their meaning as they in turn work to construct us.

The assumption that images can and should be considered texts is an oversimplification of imagery. Images are perceived holistically and for that reason may seem simpler than texts. They affect us in ways that may not be realized through simple (recognition) perception and are more highly memorable than written or verbal texts. For these reasons, images are immensely more complex than texts in their immediacy and the subtlety of their influence. Images can increase the power of text through juxtaposition and legitimate nonsensical text through apparent realism. Consider the common ad ploy aimed at girls and young women that attempts to convince them to buy things that make them all look the same, while the text of the ad promotes feelings of individualism.

In contrast to the general similarities between images and texts, images are different from texts in the ways in which they interact with human cognition (and these underlie teaching and learning). First, the ways in which *we construct images*: As Arnheim has taught us, our perception of images takes place as a gestalt. It is immediate (or very fast) and very memorable. Second, the ways in which *images construct us*: Images are inherently sensual. They are always physical and, in a sense, erotic. They attract us and make us want to look at them.

The impact of imagery's power over written text can be seen in a range of visual culture, such as advertising and television programs. Several television series and films that have aired in the United States rely at least as heavily on imagery as they do on text. This first became a characteristic style on television in shows such as the early *Mission Impossible* series, which had little talk and lots of visual effects. In *Miami Vice* (which was supposed to be the MTV of police shows), visual style was seen as a critically important element. The success of this series led to a whole genre of police, spy, and other types of shows that employ similar techniques. Action films now focus very little on dialogue and rely heavily on dramatic, fast-paced special effects and suspenseful, slowly paced motion shots.

In many television shows, films, and videos, the camera moves quickly the way our eyes might when scanning a situation—first on a face, then a hand, then an object, back to the face, and so on. Extreme closeups are used so that facial expressions become a symbolic form and are a major part of the content of the show. This style of camera work does not let us settle on any image for very long. We do not have time to become confident about what is to come in the story, which is important in the context of an audience well-versed in half-hour television plot lines. The style can have a disquieting effect. It can suggest, for example, the stress of a police interview or the excitement of a sexual encounter. But above all, it helps to create the story through images because we are forced to think in a visual manner.

The impact of imagery has a wide range of sociopolitical and economic issues which, in turn, influence students' identities, notions of citizenship, beliefs about democracy, and so on. Consider the concept of "image" not only in terms of its literal visual meaning, but also in its sense as a surface representation. As previously mentioned, from a postmodern perspective, surface is not just surface; it is deep with context and meaning. The following report by Rebecca Mead (1998) in the July 13, 1998 *New Yorker* illustrates this phenomenon:

> When lawyers from Calvin Klein filed forty-odd pages of legal documents in Manhattan Federal Court alleging that Ralph Lauren's soon-to-be-launched fragrance, Romance, would infringe upon the trademark of Calvin Klein's best-selling fragrance, Eternity, they provided a wealth of detail to support their claim. Ralph's bottle was weighty and rectangular with beveled edges, had a silvery T-shaped stopper, and bore no logo, just like Calvin's; Ralph's advertising campaign was to feature a man and a woman canoodling in outdoor settings and was to be photographed by Bruce Weber, just like Calvin's . . . What the lawyers didn't seem to think was worth mentioning was whether the two perfumes smelled alike. (Both are floral, with notes of freesia and patchouli.) This omission provides tacit confirmation of a fashion-industry fact universally acknowledged but rarely articulated, which is that when it comes to perfume, packaging is the product. The selling of fragrance is fashion logic distilled to its purest essence: the merchandise is eclipsed by its marketing. (pp. 25–26)

The point is not only made by the fashion industry. Consider all the objects designed and manufactured around other forms of popular visual culture, such as comics, cartoons, and feature films. Television cartoon series and science fiction films are now developed with the "spin-off" products in mind so that the stories will be conducive to visual culture product sales, such as those of action figures and collection cards. My students who are teachers continually bring into my classes examples of their students' own spin-offs of visual culture. These students create whole worlds derived from visual culture where their interest focuses on imagery, in part, because the stories are fairly redundant.

However, it is important to remember that "image" is not trivial; it involves large-scale, symbolic identity. From a postmodern perspective, image is deep with cultural meaning. A good illustration of the complex connection between image and meaning can be seen in the visual choices people make to reveal cultural identities. Cultural differences and identities are profoundly illustrated and supported through

the visual arts, but at the same time, the visual arts cross cultural boundaries and comment on those boundaries. Ruth Cuthand's work *Living
Post-Oka Kind of Woman* addresses conflicts of crossing cultures and
the many identities of women. Through rough drawings of a paper doll
with various outfits and text, Cuthand portrays some of the complexities of being Plains Cree and female in contemporary society. The text
above the paper doll states, "With this exciting new look, Indian can
move from the board room, to a feminist meeting, to a social function."
As Cuthand illustrates, our identities are often reflected and defined
by the ways in which we visually represent ourselves from how we dress,
to where we go, to what we watch.

Visual Representation as Didactic Form: Ads as Examples

Advertisements particularly illustrate the process of establishing meaning as inherent to aesthetics. Ads link together arbitrary sets of signifiers
(e.g., Poster, 1994; Williamson, 1978) that suggest cultural associations.
The early meaning of the term *advertisement* simply referred to the
presentation of information, as used by Shakespeare in the 16th century. In the 17th and 18th centuries, advertisements of products became
common to inform people of the product's existence. However, by the
end of the 19th century, advertisements had begun using overt psychological devices to convince, for example, through the suggestion that
one was lacking in something if one did not have the product. The so-
called lacking was intended to create feelings of desire (Williamson,
1978). However, even the informational type of advertising was intended
to influence and change behavior (Barnard, 1995).

Contemporary advertising seems quite different from, and more
powerful than, its earlier, 19th-century antecedents. Throughout the
earlier century, advertisements were mainly based on text. Contemporary advertisers use imagery far more than text. In part, they use
images because colors and shapes attract our attention, but also because they can be a particularly efficient way to communicate information. We perceive and process imagery more quickly than text and
have created technological capabilities that enable the mass production of sophisticated imagery on a large scale. Through imagery, advertisers can efficiently suggest certain associations that they hope
will cause us to make the conceptual connections necessary to make
those associations. It works if advertisers know their audience. For
example, ad images representing issues of gender and ethnicity are
largely conservative and attempt to engage their intended audience
in a relationship with characters that will be pleasurable, giving the

viewer a sense of being in control. People in a particular audience, such as those having the same sociocultural background, might tend to make the same associations about certain things they consider desirable, such as nature, youth, and sex. Advertisers hope we will be attracted to the seductive qualities of the imagery and transfer felt desire for aspects of the image to the product.

Images that advertisers hope will make desirable suggestions are connected to products and brand names through juxtapositions that are inherently didactic. Using such arbitrary links, advertisers attempt to educate people to participate in the reality they construct, so that we will act as consumers. Through messages of identity, desire, and power, ads seem to speak to individuals, while attempting to shape mass consciousness. The didactic characteristics of imagery are critical if ads are to function as they are intended.

The use of imagery to promote desire is not only seen in advertising, and the aesthetics of imagery has worked for centuries to show people what is possible, ideal, even fantastic. Advertisements can inform us about issues, ideas, and even products that are important for us to be aware of or are good for us, such as political campaign ads and the antismoking *Truth* ad campaign. What is important from the perspective of teaching visual culture is that students develop enough knowledge to make intelligent decisions about the visual culture they make and see and the ways in which visual culture will influence them.

CULTURAL AND PERSONAL INTERPRETATIONS

As well as teaching people the content of their messages, ads also teach people how to "read" ads. They contain didactic cues that educate viewers to interpret imagery in a particular manner that is quickly recognized, deeply associative, and easily internalized. Visual culture can be interpreted almost simultaneously on a general culture level and a personal level (Freedberg, 1989). Cultural readings may be intended meanings, those preferred by advertisers, while personal meaning may derive from the unintentional. Particularly in a heterogeneous society, cultural, as well as individual, readings involve levels of difference due, in part, to different cultural experiences between social, ethnic, and gender groups and the ways in which members of these groups interpret experience. And yet, the contribution of the audience is not entirely individual and unique because similar people have similar experiences from which to interpret and integrate new experience.

The Idea of Audience

In order to investigate the ways in which people interpret visual culture, and the importance of association in learning about the visual arts, an exploration of the concept of audience in communication theory can add insight. Early communication theorists, such as Adorno and Horkheimer, focused to a great extent on the sending and receiving of messages. However, approaches to the way in which images are received and understood that focus on either artist or audience are implausible because they do not take into account the complex social conditions of the process (Morley, 1992). The process is more likely a highly interactive relationship between imagery and audience that is both similar and different for individuals and groups (e.g., Best & Kellner, 1991; Morley, 1992; Thompson, 1994). The appropriation and use of information (which is a form of cognition) by audiences is given attention in current theory about the suggestiveness of signs. Based on hermeneutics, this poststructural approach to audience involvement emerged from considerations of the reading of literary texts in relation to individual, lived experiences. In contrast to the earlier view that an author controls the message that will be taken from a text, recent theory has attended to the importance of interpretation, for example, in relation to history (Jauss, 1982), authoritative communities (Fish, 1982), and use (Eagleton, 1983).

Advertisements illustrate the process of establishing meaning for audiences in relation to the interpretation of signs. The arbitrary sets of written and pictorial signifiers carry with them certain cultural associations. In a commercial, images that people associate with nature, youth, and sex are combined with a soft drink, deodorant, or detergent. Such an arbitrary link does not refer back to some reality, but instead creates a new reality, or *hyperreality*, that is didactic. Using such juxtapositions, advertisers attempt to educate people to think in the context of the reality they construct. With these images, advertisers not only sell products; they sell politics. At the same time that ads attempt to shape mass consciousness, advertisers seem to speak to individuals through messages of identity, desire, and power.

The new world of technology and the blurred boundaries of culture have made popular culture increasingly pedagogical (Giroux & Simon, 1989). Beach and Freedman's (1992) study of adolescents' appropriation of advertising representations of gender demonstrated that students often conceptually locate themselves in ads and even used the fictional world in the ad as a standard against which reality should be judged. This study indicated that students do not view images critically unless they are specifically taught how to do so. As a result, their appropriation from images can result in knowledge (such as gender stereotypes) that is inconsistent with democratic goals of schooling (such as equity).

Few educators would argue against the idea that students need to develop good critical skills and that citizens in a democracy should consider these skills essential to good citizenship. And yet, visual culture can work to shape audiences in ways that can confound critique and allow students to be uncritical observers. Good students of visual culture make informed decisions in all their roles as members of an audience, as producers, as artists, and so on.

Images of Art: The Example of Fine Art in the Mass Media

In this section, the social construction of ideas about fine art is discussed through the example of representation in the mass media as a type of curriculum content that can illustrate how visual culture works back upon itself. Filmmakers use graphic devices, such as composition, color scheme, and design; and reference other forms of art through the use of art styles such as neorealism, expressionism, or surrealism. They recycle fine art and architecture through the design of scenery, lighting, costumes, face and figure selection (casting), and various photographic techniques. They also combine these devices with fragments of historical and fictional accounts of fine art, such as a biographical sketch of an artist, the creation of a masterpiece, or action located in a museum. They juxtapose these fragments in a way different from reality, creating a new reality in the process.

The post-World War II emergence of an American fascination with the fine art community was reflected in popular film and television. After World War II, American art educators shifted their attention to teaching children about what fine artists, and other members of the fine art community, do in their professional capacities. Public attention also focused on artists' personalities and personal lives, particularly those who had highly fictionalized biographies, such as Michelangelo, Toulouse-Lautrec, and Van Gogh. The representations of these artists in film helped to shape people's conceptions of art.

Multiple, contradictory meanings are inherently suggested by representations (Derrida, 1976). This can be illustrated by the ways in which artists are represented as having chaotic studios and lives, as unconcerned about their own physical appearance and the chaos around them, and yet immersed in the appearance of their art. To produce order from chaos makes the production seem all the more important and difficult. The chaos is supposedly in an artist's mind, as well as in the physical world. Artists are represented as struggling heroically with the unseen demons of madness, and yet are considered gifted by characters and audience. Artists are seen as having control over nothing but their work, and even their art is just beyond their reach at times. They create, but art has a life of its own. To produce art takes hard work and discipline. Yet art appears through an artist's body, in uncontrollable spurts, sometimes when the artist least expects it, and at any time of the day or night—certainly not only within regular working hours.

These representations enslave and glorify artists, are reproduced by artists, and serve broad cultural purposes. "The artist" in popular media is a mythological character created, in part, to symbolize public and private ideals of Western culture. Artists are signs of private desires of sexuality and freedom, and yet representations of artists suggest public achievement and enlightenment, even beyond knowledge and reason. Artists are represented as extremely emotional people who push the limits of society, take chances, and do things others would not dare. Artists' sexuality is considered so closely connected to their art that they have been considered promiscuous by nature or by profession. They have no shame, because they answer to some higher calling that elevates them above common people and common values. In contrast, artists are also represented as existing on a high moral plane and working in the service of a great force that is inherently good. Many representations of premodern artists have focused on religious fervor tied to a gift of artistic talent from God. Representations of modern artists have shifted in focus to a secular type of higher calling, such as art for art's sake (art defined as inherently good) or individual self-expression (defined as good through associations with psychological health and a democratic political milieu).

American popular culture about fine art has been largely produced from a modernist perspective that promotes the idea of extreme individualism. Artists are represented as creating entirely unique ideas in a mind separated from society, while at the same time doing what is best for society. We tend to be shown the artist at work or surrounded by work; that is, the artist in his or her medium. In part, this physical environment highlights the artists' struggle with the isolation that is assumed to come with artistic creation. Images of an artist surrounded by his or her work may suggest that the work is his or her intermediary with the world.

From 1950 to 1965, a number of serious and comic Hollywood films focused on fine art as important parts of their plots. Some of these films were based on biographies of artists, which were also popular reading at the time. The plots were of two major types. One type was a serious film about psychological struggles for individualism and independence by famous pre-20th-century artists. The second type of film was often comic and focused upon a representation of fictional contemporary artists who did not want to do real work and conned the public with abstract and nonobjective images while living a Bohemian lifestyle. The comic films also represented artists as alienated from society, but for different reasons. The artist-heroes in the dramatic films tended to be alienated by genius (and a slightly unbalanced mind). Genius was their character flaw because it prevented them from functioning normally in mainstream society. The artist characters in the comedies were usually flawed by laziness and dishonesty. Interestingly, the art produced by these comedic characters often superficially resembled Jackson Pollack's drip paintings.

Dramatic films of the 1950s and 1960s represented art as a struggle for excellence, a reflection of genius, and an ideal that maintained and yet progressively transformed culture. The (specifically male) artist-hero fought against all odds to express himself, benefit humanity, and find or create truth. At the same time, the artist was represented as mentally unstable, antisocial, and egotistical. This shows how art signifies what is culturally valuable, but also what is ignored, ridiculed, and idiosyncratic.

The second type of postwar representation of art in popular media can be found in television and film comedies. The irreverence of the avant-garde (and particularly abstract expressionism) was played upon in several comedies in the 1950s and 1960s. The fine art community was represented as conning the public in films like *Bikini Beach* (1964) with Annette Funicello and Frankie Avalon through images of art critics proclaiming paint throwing an act of genius, artists selling the work of monkeys and children, and "masterpieces" created through spills and other mishaps.

Students with whom I have worked at several educational levels have found such diverse representations of a single concept or issue to be helpful in developing an understanding of the ways in which representations work and interpretations develop based on prior and extended knowledge. As part of their historical study they can generally extend knowledge by contributing their own contemporary examples to lessons. Infusing examples from various visual arts enables students to see historical connections between types of images and objects that go across visual culture forms that have often been ignored in curriculum.

CONCLUSION

The representational character of and relationships between various forms of visual culture are an important part of cultural knowledge and influence student interpretation both in terms of art making and viewing. Cultural knowledge is reconstituted in a classroom through curriculum. The ways in which visual culture presents us with challenges of knowledge construction can be addressed in curriculum through the following interacting approaches:

1. The ability to interpret and respond to global visual culture in a sophisticated manner is essential in the contemporary world. *Response is a cultural and a personal act.* Culture is the medium within which response, including the response of making art, is suspended. Individual response is often made up of cultural associations as well as unique ideas, opinions, and beliefs. Artistic practices are communal acts as well as the actions of a single individual.

2. A conceptual "space" exists between objects, images, texts, and other art forms within which possibilities exist for learning. The aesthetic of contemporary visual culture is based, in part, on *intertextuality and intergraphicality* (the perceptual cross-fertilization of images and artifacts). When studying professional fine art and other visual culture, the study is enriched by making references to other cultural forms, which is aided through newer technologies.

3. Curriculum will need to be based, in part, on *suggestiveness* as a means of student knowledge construction. If we want students to think critically about global technologies, we should actively engage them in ways to decipher suggestions of meaning. Students must learn to interrogate both intended meanings and the meanings they construct. Students' participation and creativity involved in constructing knowledge from *suggested* meaning should be made clear. If we want students to think critically about visual culture, they need to actively engage in reflecting on their own art and their responses to postmodern culture (what they are, where they came from, how they relate to experience, and so on).

4. References to knowledge come from a variety of sources outside of school (not only the professional community of the art world). These fragmented, often contradictory, multidisciplinary, and intercultural references may have more to do with student understanding of a subject than does curriculum based on the structure of a discipline. As a result, *border conflicts and connections between bodies of knowledge* through making and viewing will become ever more important in curriculum.

5. Art education should help students reflect on the seductive power of visual culture so that they become aware of the continual learning that is part of their daily contact with it. The *epistemological instability* reflected in postmodern imagery and objects requires students to become conscious of the ways in which they construct their own knowledge through their encounters with forms of visual culture.

CHAPTER 6

Curriculum as Process

Visual Culture and Democratic Education

CURRICULUM REFLECTS PEOPLE'S HOPES AND DREAMS. It represents expectations, mediates cultural knowledge, and is intended to communicate our best thinking to our fellow human beings. Therefore, it is a form of social action. Theorizing visual culture in educational settings, designing and implementing educational plans, and evaluating art educational programming are all part of the social process by way of which we present the many aspects of visual forms of representation to students. If we choose, we can promote ideals that have been important to the arts and to democratic curriculum, such as intellectual freedom, creative imagination, and social responsibility. As a result, the power of students' and teachers' ideas and opinions expressed and interpreted through visual forms is being given new attention in curriculum. Sure, fashion designers are free to try to convince us to pay for their advertising by wearing brand names; but we are free to provide an education that will help students to make informed decisions about their visual culture choices.

These dynamics of freedom that surround visual culture in a democracy suggest that synthesizing concepts for inclusion in curriculum can be a challenge. They illustrate that the old assertion that democratic education was to simply provide equal access to excellence (i.e., masterpieces) falls short in contemporary democracies. From the perspective of teaching visual culture, the assertion only serves to promote the values of a small, rich elite. Contemporary curriculum involves more complex systems of freedom, individualism, equity, and social responsibility. The idea of democratic curriculum has long focused on individualism, at least since the work of John Dewey (1916/

1944). But for Dewey, the individual mind was understood as taking part in critical and reflective inquiry within the social and physical world. The focus on individualism in art also grew after the Second World War as people became increasingly concerned about the possible authoritarian effects of education on children in a democracy. Following the believed effects of authoritarianism and socialism on the German people and Nazi allies, these concerns were powerful in their influence over education in the United States.

Several other characteristics of democratic curriculum have emerged through educational discussions and debates. Democratic curriculum enables the critique of its own philosophical position and its process as a part of the social world (Griffin, 1996). By the 1960s, when an increased interest in discipline-based education emerged, in part as a result of international competition in the scientific communities, a focus grew on decision-making in curriculum (Engle, 1960) and on productive and creative thought (Taba & Elzey, 1964). Connections were made between higher-order thinking and public value conflicts in students' minds, binding the importance of student decision-making in curriculum to the development of democratic thought (Oliver & Shaver, 1966). The increasing focus on the role of curriculum in shaping student thought and society in the post-World War II 1950s and 1960s and the use of European critical theory in curriculum analyses during the 1970s and 1980s led to reconsiderations of the social aspects of curriculum. The connection of higher-order thinking and public value conflicts became important to establish in students' minds (Oliver & Shaver, 1966), and the possibility of including these in curriculum is an illustration of the freedoms of a democratic society. Curriculum was to aid student understanding of the conditions of democracy and the importance of cultural context to this understanding.

As part of an understanding of the importance of teaching cultural contexts in general education, Michael Apple (1975) and other scholars have argued that democratic curriculum includes teaching conflicts, including those concerning debates within professional communities (Graff, 1987). The discussion of controversial issues by students in an open intellectual climate is associated with higher levels of political interest, efficacy, and knowledge. These conflicts can also help students to understand concepts such as justice through the consideration of moral dilemmas by diverse groups (Kohlberg, 1981). Measures of democratization for use in curriculum evaluation include levels of participation and contestation (Dahl, 1971), transformation

(Giroux, 1992), and respect for difference and common ground (Beyer & Liston, 1996).

POSTMODERN CURRICULUM

From a postmodern perspective, these democratic principles of curriculum are valued, but even concepts previously considered fairly stable are in flux. As a result, postmodern curriculum acknowledges that democratic principles are ideals, but are difficult to achieve in practice. In considerations of curriculum content, time loses its neat linearity, cultural spaces seem to expand and contract, and boundaries of various sorts are blurred. Postmodern art makes imperative a connectedness that undermines knowledge as traditionally taught in school, highlighting the importance of interactions between individuals, cultural groups, forms of representation, and professional disciplines.

Changes in Curriculum Theory

Recently, curriculum theorists have been struggling with ways in which to reconceptualize curriculum from a postmodern perspective. This project has become critical as societies and cultures leave the secure thinking of modernistic forms of education where knowledge is represented as stable and curriculum is intended to be reproductive. Postmodern curriculum theorists point out that curriculum is not a neutral enterprise. It contains the interests of individuals and social groups and that these interests should made visible. For example, curriculum theorist Patrick Slattery (1995) argues that curriculum expresses autobiography because it is created by people who leave parts of themselves in their teaching and writing. He suggests that curriculum should focus on issues of the self, because that is where learning takes place, and that educators can use autobiography to better understand educational conditions. Slattery's understanding of curriculum is an example of a renewed awakening to the aesthetics of education.

Another change in the ways in which curriculum is understood by theorists has to do with the total curriculum process. Rather than being only a single written text, curriculum is conceived as a process through which students learn. Conceptualized as a process, curriculum can refer to the ways in which students learn outside, as well as inside of classrooms or institutions, and the intended part of the curriculum process may change as the curriculum is enacted. Within classrooms and institutions, the hidden curriculum (Jackson, 1968)—that which is learned outside of the intentions of the teacher, such as stereotypes—is also an important part of the learning experience. The null curriculum (Eisner, 1979) is the important knowledge that a student does not learn because it is left out of school, such as when art is not included in a school program. It also plays a role in shaping student understanding of the world.

As a result of such emphases in curriculum, an art classroom may be seen as a technical work environment, rather than as a broadly based area of intellectual pursuit. Of course, the technical aspects of art (such as manipulation of materials and formal qualities) are important, but the conceptual side of art—the ideas, imagination, style, and so on— can only grow when cultivated through enriching social environments. Psychologist Donald Norman (1993) discusses the problem in relation to environments that inappropriately focus on technology that narrows thinking rather than expanding it.

> People are effective when they work in a rich, varied environment. A disembodied intelligence is deprived of rich sources of information . . . some aspects of technology expose us to demands for accuracy and precision that are of little importance to normal life. Nonetheless, we have altered our lives to give in to the machine-centered focus on high accuracy, even where accuracy is not critical. Our goal should be to develop human-centered activities, to make environment and the task fit the person, not the other way around. (Norman, 1993, p. 153)

Norman's lesson for art education is not that curriculum should be devoid of technology, but that we have shifted the focus of life so much to the qualities of things that their meanings may escape us. We must be wary of curriculum that focuses on the technical aspects of art and on "accurate" interpretations.

Five Conditions of the Curriculum Process

At least five conditions illustrate this reconceptualization of curriculum as process, and these conditions, at least symbolically, refer to conditions of postmodern aesthetics. First, curriculum is a form of representation. It embodies, in ephemeral and concrete ways, the hopes and dreams of people as well as what they know. As such, it is not only a matter of knowledge per se, but of the shape of knowledge formed in relation to values, beliefs, and social structures. It represents less of what artists, authors, and scientists actually do than philosophies about those activities and thought processes (Apple, 1972). Although we do our best to develop logical sequences of experience through which students are to learn concepts and skills, curriculum is highly selective, has blurred boundaries, and is unpredictable.

Second, curriculum is like a collage. Anthropologist James Clifford's (1988) conception of ethnographic studies of culture can help us to understand the social problem of curriculum. He speaks of culture as a collage of many cultural identities that are selected and translated on a continuing basis. Far from being a unified whole, any particular culture is a combination of others, with its resulting contradictions and incongruities. The forms of curriculum production (curriculum theorizing, research, and implementation) have similar collagelike qualities. They are made of multiple contributions, from various sources, with competing interests. They involve a cut-and-pasted construction of the ideas of individuals and groups. The ideas are selected and brought together, with care and a sense of unease, to form a whole. As Slattery (1995) argues, bits of the people who, for example, create new knowledge, write curriculum, and teach are part of that whole.

Third, curriculum is a creative production. It is sketched, formed, and enacted and it continually changes as it is implemented, criticized, and revised. Educators write articles and books based on disciplined inquiry; design curriculum based on books, articles, and other curricula; and implement curriculum through teaching. Students and teachers interpret curriculum, conduct disciplined inquiry based on what they have learned, and so on. Regardless of the degree to which curriculum is "centralized," it is influenced by the constraints of its institutional medium, the talents of its actors, and at any given moment, the vision of its subject. Researchers and theorists who study and attempt to understand the ways in which curriculum works argue that we can no longer maintain the belief that what we put on paper and call "a curriculum" is the whole story. Acts of teaching and learning are part of the process of curriculum. It is a translation of knowledge into information that is selected, organized, and interpreted by the curriculum developer, which is then taught to students through another interpretation, which will be reinterpreted by the students as they create their own knowledge.

Fourth, curriculum suggests what Clifford (1988) calls "likely stories," rather than objectified and disembodied truth. As such, it can be conceptualized as an interaction between teachers, students, and a range of texts and images. Modernist curriculum often appears to subordinate the details of each part and directs students toward a single, positive knowledge. In contrast, a postmodern approach could make the creative process of curriculum more transparent so that students understand it as a highly complex matter of bringing together and making sense out of dissonant qualities. Curriculum could be seen as a collagelike combination of information—like other aspects of life—which is necessarily ambiguous and suggestive of multiple meanings. It is a vital part of lived experience. We put it together as if telling a story or creating a painting—to make internal sense—but it is necessarily ambiguous and can never exactly reproduce ideas in the professional field. So that curriculum makes internal sense within the confines of institutions, we are forced to simplify and technicize information from the disciplines, often losing or hiding its deeper meanings, but in the process we open up possibilities for reconceptualizing knowledge by leaving holes in arguments and gaps between facts that must be newly argued or theorized.

Fifth, curriculum should be made transparent. To make curriculum transparent is a matter of revealing to students the ways in which curriculum is constituted through the actions of conducting research, reporting, "reading," and otherwise interpreting, planning and writing, and enacting, including the ways in which individual teachers come to understand curriculum structures and content and present these in class. Such transparency can be advantageous to students who can engage with curriculum at a level other than mere reception and who can begin to reflect upon processes of teaching and learning. Through curriculum inquiry, students' construction of knowledge can be enhanced as they work with teachers to take part in these processes. If, for example, we accept the view that the teaching of art should help students to establish meaning in their lives, then we need to make our purposes clear to them and the ways in which they can establish meaning should be included as part of curriculum.

REPRESENTING VISUAL CULTURE
IN CURRICULUM STRUCTURES

As a result of the scientific rhetoric discussed in Chapter 1, the relationship between educational aims (the larger interests of education), goals (the middle-level interests of school curriculum), and learning objectives (the particular interests of a lesson) can represent art in inappropriate ways. Figure 6.1 illustrates examples of curriculum aims and goals. Many different objectives could be written to meet these goals. While the aims of education might be expressed in a language that represents visual culture in an appropriate manner, an increasing dependence on artificial separation of disciplines and scientific rhetoric as the educational purposes get closer to the classroom (and to assessment) results in their technization. For example, high school art curriculum often includes learning objectives with a narrow focus on

Figure 6.1. Examples of curriculum aims and goals.

AIMS:
Societal focus—what are the social values and purposes of the curriculum as a whole?

GOALS:
Institutional or political unit focus—what should the curriculum enable or provide to fulfill the above aims?

Examples of curriculum aims and goals:

Aim #1:   To promote the development of a democratic population.
Goal #1:   Multicultural sensitivity.

Aim #2:   To promote responsible care of the natural environment.
Goal #2:   Ecological awareness.

Aim #3:   To promote the creation of new knowledge.
Goal #3:   Creative production.

media skills or the elements and principles of design. That is, the objectives are based on simple formal or technical skills that are easily taught and assessed, but are disconnected from the complexity appropriate to instruction for students at this age.

Eisner (e.g., 1973/1974) has argued that curriculum should include expressive objectives that emerge from an educational experience as well as instructional objectives that are to predict behavior. He states:

> The expressive objective is an outcome realized by the student after having engaged in an activity that was intended to generate a personal idiosyncratic response . . . the instructional objective is prescriptive, and the instructional activity is not a prescription of what it will take to achieve it. The expressive activity is not prescriptive; it is evocative. It does not seek to anticipate what kind of particular response or product the students produce. Instead it aims at constructing an encounter, creating a setting, forming a situation which will stimulate diverse and largely unanticipated responses and solutions from students. What students learn from such encounters becomes—post-facto—the expressive objective. (1973/1974, p. 190)

The conflict between educational rhetoric and the goals of art education is illustrated when learning objectives are enacted. Objectives can be planned, but important learning outcomes cannot always be predicted and, in art education, the best outcomes are often those that are beyond "the box" of the objectives in their creativity, imaginativeness, and originality. Art problems are authentic; they are some of the few problems in school for which the teacher does not know the answer. They are sociocultural, as well as psychobiological, and will unpredictably cross disciplinary borders.

Forms of Curriculum for Planning and Design

Several forms of curriculum should be included in instructional planning and design. None of the forms of curriculum should be used as the only form of curriculum because each contains strengths and serves different purposes. These forms include: *sequential curriculum, interactive curriculum, event experiences*, and *interdisciplinary curriculum*.

Sequential Curriculum. A program that is sequenced builds on previous knowledge from the educational program. Several types of sequential plans exist. For example, a sequential program may be *linear*, may be conceptualized as *building blocks*, or may resemble a *spiral*. A linear curriculum is cumulative, so that each lesson presents new information that adds to previous content. A building block program involves a gradual increase of both amount and conceptual level of content. A spiral program builds on knowledge not only by advancing information to an increasing and more sophisticated level, but by revisiting the same concepts and skills to promote rehearsal. Each of these types of sequence may be beneficial depending on the concepts and skills intended to be taught. A linear form of curriculum might be helpful when merely adding to students' repertoire of painting techniques. A building block approach can be used when attempting to increase and advance the conceptual complexity of student understanding of a particular painting style. This could be done, for example, by studying an increasing number of historical artists who painted in that style and increasing the complexity of the study by enlarging the sphere of the artists' social context and relating it to their art. A spiral curriculum involves practicing skills and concepts at given intervals over time and increasing the level of complexity at each rehearsal. A spiral curriculum is complex in its organization because each review is intended to increase knowledge as well as reinforce it. So, at each rehearsal students could newly make conceptual connections between their painting, the paintings of historical artists, the artists' contexts, and the students' contexts. Of these types of sequential curriculum, a spiral plan is most appropriate for teaching the complexities of visual culture.

Interactive Curriculum. This form of curriculum involves responsive programming tuned to students' experience outside of school. This is a form of negotiated curriculum, which should be developed through contributions from students and, as a result of this mutually "owned" content, helps to create a learning culture that extends beyond the classroom. It may involve art learning that students undergo outside of the sequence of planned activities of the intended curriculum and may respond to hidden curriculum issues. For example, lessons may be introduced concerning gender stereotypes that may appear in student work or be included because a student raised questions about pornography in class. Interactive curriculum addresses contemporary issues as they emerge and responds to change as it occurs. It may attend to a television series the students are watching at home or a film that has initiated student interest in a range of other visual culture products, enriching meaning in art learning through life experience. This form of curriculum is to help students connect art knowledge they learn outside of school with knowledge that students want to learn and educators hope they will learn.

Event Experiences. Event experiences bring into curriculum highly memorable events, such as a museum visit or art performance. Event experiences can provide students and teachers with an extraordinary common memory and a shared discourse on which to build knowledge as a community. Although such events may not be part of sequential curriculum, they can be powerful learning experiences because students often remember these special events as provoking a high level of interest and because they are separate from their day-to-day experience. Such events include attending a performance, seeing a gallery or museum exhibition, working with an artist-in-residence in the school, attending a feature film, or visiting a commercial art business or television studio. The project related to such an event can come before or after the event, but should tie the event to ongoing learning by highlighting the range of art skills and concepts that students learn through the event.

Interdisciplinary Curriculum. Art is inherently interdisciplinary and art curriculum should include content that integrates knowledge traditionally separated in various school subjects. In the past, concern has existed among art educators that interdisciplinary curriculum would threaten art education and allow art to be used only to support other school subjects. Unquestionably, the concern has been supported by historical evidence when art has been totally infused into curriculum. However, the relevance of visual culture is challenged when it is taught in esoteric ways that isolate objects from their social meanings. Appropriately responding to the concern is not a matter of denying that visual culture should be taught from an interdisciplinary perspective, but rather answering the questions of when, where, and how to integrate knowledge across disciplines. For example, reading, writing, and making should be included in all art courses, but it is appropriate that some lessons focus on one of these more than the others. A great deal of work is needed by teachers and researchers in the field to begin to answer the questions of when, where, and how integration should occur.

In order to promote the construction of a range of art knowledge, curriculum development should start with key concepts rather than activities, and increase its focus on technical skills as students reach the end of high school and go into higher education. Unfortunately, many of the students who take an elective art class in high school will never take another formal art class, and yet these are often the classes designed to focus on basic technical skills rather than the important aspects of art that students will use for the rest of their lives. It is the students who go on to the higher-level art classes in high school, those who think of becoming professional artists, who learn about the important ideas of art—but most students never get there (and then people wonder why art is so little valued in school). An important question is, What concepts and skills concerning visual culture are important enough to spend the little time on that we have with our students? A list of some of those concepts can be found in the example scope and sequence in Figure 6.2. It is built on a spiral model of curriculum so that the concepts are revisited with increasing complexity at each higher level. However, it is only one possibility and should be approached with a view to flexibility and support from the other forms of curriculum.

Social Responsibility and Educational Leadership

Students have always been involved with the social functions of art, even when the topic was not considered in an overt and reflective manner. As has been argued here, no other part of education can help students understand the power of the visual arts in human life or so well explain the interactive relationship between cognition and emotion, thinking and feeling. To talk of student art may give the impression of a politically neutral health maintenance and vocational training, but art education is clearly tied to the political aspects (citizenship, science, gender, etc.) of social life. Through art education, students are introduced to the rich heritage of world visual culture, not only to expand

Figure 6.2. Example scope and sequence for teaching visual culture.

ORGANIZER	PRIMARY LEVEL	MIDDLE LEVEL	HIGH SCHOOL LEVEL	HIGHER ED. FOUNDATIONS
1. SOCIETY	Art is made by and for people.	Art has many social purposes and contexts.	Art has social, political, and economic conditions.	Art is a form of social production.
2. IMAGINATION	People use their imaginations to create art.	Art involves imagining forms of ideas and emotions.	Art is created through the imaginative use of metaphor, symbol, and related concepts.	High-level visualization and creation requires broad knowledge and reflexivity in the use of imagination.
3. POINT OF VIEW/ STANCE	Art suggests a point of view.	Through the expression of a point of view in their work, artists can take a stand.	Point of view or stance determines choice and handling of subject matter and the interpretations of those choices.	Art professionals philosophically position themselves through the stance(s) of their creations and interpretations.
4. INTERPRETATION	Different people interpret art differently.	Art asks questions that have many possible answers, but some are more supportable than others.	Interpretation of art enables audiences to make cognitive connections that personalize and extend meaning.	Complex meaning develops through various interpretive filters that enable sophisticated reflection and analysis.
5. IDENTITY	Each person makes art about himself/herself and his/her world.	Art helps people construct and become conscious of identity.	Individual and cultural identities are constructed and revealed through art.	Art is a personal statement, in a cultural context, with an individual style.
6. CULTURE	The people of each culture make art in their own way.	Art is central to the development of cultures and subcultures, including student subcultures.	Art is a cultural carrier; it is shaped by cultural conditions and reveals them.	Art, and its professional communities, promote cultural reification and critique.
7. MEDIATION	People tell stories through art.	Through artistic narration and representation, people communicate with each other.	People mediate knowledge, attitudes, beliefs, and behaviors through art.	Art mediates other cultural forms, connecting people and cultures, past and present.

8. PAST/PRESENT	People have always made art.	Some aspects of art change over time, while other aspects stay the same.	Both history, and people's responses to history, are important to art.	Art professionals challenge history in the development of contemporary thought.
9. FORM	People design art.	Making art requires the knowledgeable use of formal qualities.	Creativity is nurtured through the practice of formal techniques and processes.	Art professionals learn accepted formal rules and when to break those rules.
10. MEDIUM	People make art using a variety of materials.	Craftsmanship relies on technical skills and an understanding of media properties.	Media skills mature through practice and the conscious use of media properties.	High-level media skills include the ability to push media to their extremes.
11. INQUIRY	People make art based on what they see and what they know.	Investigation and experimentation are often important to art making.	Making and understanding art depends on persistent deliberation.	Professional development in art is a process of disciplined inquiry.
12. CRITICISM	People value art for many reasons.	Art is judged against many (social, formal, etc.) criteria, which are often publicly debated.	Artistic preferences and critical perspectives are culturally as well as individually formed.	High-level art criticism depends on interdisciplinary knowledge of past and present.
13. CONTEXTS	Art is a part of everyday life.	Art shapes the environment as it shapes our conceptions of environment.	Contexts are important to understanding art, its interactions and influences.	Important relationships exist among art forms and between art and other forms of culture.
14. REFLECTIVE PRACTICE	Art can make people think.	Advanced thinking skills are important to making and viewing art.	Critical thinking about art is necessary for reflective practice.	Reflective practice is developed and sustained through professional communities.
15. DIDACTICS	Art educates.	Art can inform, persuade, and stereotype in the ways that it represents.	The influence of art is an important consideration in making life choices.	Art professionals often consider the ethics of their decisions about art.

their knowledge and to extend their imaginations, but to construct their identities. If we accept the idea that art education is actually part of identity construction, that it focuses, after all, on cultural and personal forms of interpretation and representation that influence the way in which students see themselves and the world, the responsibility of art educators becomes great indeed.

Much of the time spent by art educators on leadership issues is spent on advocacy. Art programs are often threatened in educational institutions when resources are scarce, promoting the mistaken assumption that art is a frill and an unnecessary part of human development. In cultural institutions, such as museums, educational programs are underfunded and continually challenged to maintain credibility, although one of the roles of educational programming in these institutions is to educate young people to become future audiences (which allows these institutions to continue). In these institutions, young audiences should be considered with the same seriousness that personal computer companies considered them when they gave away free computers to schools to begin the development of computer literacy and instill a desire to work with computers. After all, most of the charters of the major museums in the U.S. state that education is a goal of the institution.

Advocacy is an important part of leadership in art education, but it is not the sum total of leadership responsibilities. In a democratic society, leadership includes working in professional associations and other communities. Membership in professional groups can support art educators who sometimes feel isolated and reveal new horizons of action for school change, providing an environment for the generation and critique of ideas and practices. These groups can be small or large and should be maintained at all levels, from local groups of colleagues within an educational setting to state, national, and international organizations.

CURRICULUM CONNECTIONS, COGNITIVE CONNECTIONS

Curriculum can aid in the development of new knowledge both by presenting new information and by connecting it to prior knowledge. Teaching visual culture can serve students best by promoting enriching engagement in activities that reflect life experiences and provoke several levels of thought. Students can begin to understand how knowledge is constructed through socially interactive experiences that focus them on creating meanings, as well as products. Social educational experiences, such as cooperative learning, advance knowledge beyond expected levels precisely because they do not involve a synthetic sequence of information.

The relationships between images and their interdisciplinary connections, including the sociopolitical conditions under which they are produced and seen, are vital to understanding visual culture. This understanding is a form of cognitive appropriation through which students transform information into something they can use. People are capable of recalling and integrating a vast array of images and their associated meanings. Student artistic production is a visual illustration of this conceptual integration. When making or viewing a new visual form, the focus of cognition often involves the establishment of connections between and among dispersed references to representations of visual culture.

This is one of the many reasons that curriculum should allow students to cross over the traditional boundaries of art learning based on media techniques and processes. Most high school and higher education curriculum continues to be based on a model in which each course focuses on a single medium. This model is supported by the argument that students need to develop sophisticated skills in a single medium in order to have a thorough knowledge of the range of possibilities the medium provides, thus enabling students to express themselves more effectively. I know from personal experience that teaching a single medium–based course is easiest and the enrichment of knowledge through depth is certainly a reasonable argument. But students must simultaneously be helped to deepen their ideas as they develop their media skills and these ideas may need to cross media in their development. Contemporary fine artists and other visual culture producers do not work in a single medium as much as artists did in the past; and even when working in a single production area, such as photography or printmaking, multimedia are often used. As a result, thematic courses can often enrich student learning of visual culture better than single media-based courses.

Although the study of visual culture inherently focuses on a consideration of objects, it does not have to begin with a focus on the object per se. To start with the object may suggest to students that the milieu of the work before its creation and its life since its creation is unimportant. Rather, instruction can start with the people or context in which and for which it was produced and extend far beyond the work itself. In this way, students can develop an understanding of the conditions (cultural, social, political, economic, environmental, etc.) that made the production of the object possible and the study of it worthwhile. As indicated in Chapter 3, this represents a significant change in curriculum.

Another important change in curriculum is required when teaching visual culture. Often, in the past, students have been left to develop their artistic production work over many days without being required to develop new knowledge. This is the case because art has typically been taught based on the studio model of an individual fine artist, who has already developed a personal and cultural reservoir of concepts, rather than being based on the idea of a learning community. It is assumed that students will necessarily construct new knowledge in the process of doing production activities, and although they may develop new skills, they may not enrich their conceptual knowledge. To teach visual culture effectively, including when students are in the process of making art, requires that new concepts and/or skills are taught each day so that students are able to connect a range of types of knowledge to their production. This involves some collaboration between and among students so that the sum of students' knowledge can be used to the advantage of individuals and so that students understand that individual, professional artists draw on the work of their peers. It also means that teachers should simplify information given at the front end of lessons and add complexity as the lesson continues. For example, instead of a long lecture on fine art history before a series of classes only involving artistic production, concepts and skills will need to be pulled out, infused, and reinforced throughout the lesson so that students can construct and connect knowledge as they rehearse it through their art making. This can be done by briefly teaching a new concept or skill every day through additional skill training as it is needed in the process of completion of a student work of art, by building conceptual complexity through the introduction of related concepts as a lesson progresses, or by including the work of diverse artists and various forms of visual culture as new examples of previously taught concepts within a lesson.

Becoming Aware of Conceptual Links

Forms of visual culture cross paths and in the process extend and suggest new meanings. Works of fine art that have become icons, such as DaVinci's *Mona Lisa*, Michelangelo's *David*, Munch's *Scream*, and Wood's *American Gothic*, have crossed several boundaries of form over the years and, as a result, have played a part in more levels of aesthetic experience than they would have if seen exclusively in a single venue. Artistic styles, such as French impressionism, are commonly recycled and transformed. Impressionism was considered scandalous by the fine art academy in its infancy, became accepted as an important foundation of fine art, and is now commonly seen as part of popular visual culture. Likewise, popular culture images and objects are often literally and figuratively reused in various ways.

In part, knowledge construction takes place through *intertextuality* in which references are made by a "reader" to various other texts the person has read in the past. Intertextuality might be said to take place in the conceptual space between texts. Rather than focusing only on the text at hand, meaningful reading focuses on contexts, and therefore, on the connections between various (written and verbal) texts. If this were not the case, we would have to learn new things in order to understand each new text that we read, we would not be able to relate one text to another, and text producers would not be able to use techniques like simile, analogy, and metaphor.

The same type of conceptual space exists for visual culture that provides a milieu for connections to develop between the range of images we see (Freedman, 1994). Through this *intergraphicality*, our minds are capable of recalling and integrating a vast array of images and their associated meanings. Cognition involves reference to interactions between dispersed references to various forms of representations. The images we have encountered in the past become attached to associations related to the context in which we saw them, including the context of thoughts about or the conceptual space between previous experiences. In a sense, the attached meanings are part of what is known about the images until we restructure or construct new knowledge through more experience. This process, then, enables us to comingle images, make associations between them, recycle and change them, as we restructure knowledge and create new images and art.

Studies of learning transfer have been done to investigate questions of prior knowledge. However, educational researcher Lauren Resnick (1994) argues that the notions of individual differences and learning transfer may defeat the good intentions of educators, including those who are concerned with crossing disciplinary boundaries. This might be the case because information does not actually transfer per se across domain-specific areas of the brain. Instead, what may appear as transfer are multiple cognitive connections determined by the ways in which individuals uniquely respond to situations in which concepts and skills are developed. As Resnick explains,

> Both of these constructs have been classically defined in terms of bundles of relatively stable skills. Over the decades, debate has focused on how to describe these skills and how they bundle together. The situated ratio-

nalist framework suggests that, instead of decontextualized skills, it would be helpful to think of *personal histories* as the important determinants of the way an individual will act in a particular situation. (p. 490, emphasis in original)

Resnick points out that the "situations experienced as similar to a past situation will initially evoke—not necessarily consciously—ways of behaving that developed through practice and tuning in the previous situation" (p. 490). If these behaviors work—that is, they result in some kind of success—they are practiced and elaborated. Transfer, then, might be thought of as a previous way of doing something that works successfully in a new situation. In art education, the impact of such collateral experience shapes learning even at the most basic emotional level of comfort with unfamiliar art (Smith-Shank, 1995). The challenge for art educators is to develop curriculum that promotes these aspects of learning.

The Importance of Conceptual Conflict

Curriculum shapes what students know and how they come to know. Therefore, attention to developmental considerations in curriculum concerns not only the organization of content for schoolwork. It also involves juxtapositions of language practices, cultural norms and ideals, student experience, and other social conditions that can influence the ways in which students restructure knowledge. For example, a commonly practiced belief is that students' lives outside of school are left at the classroom door and teachers should overcome student experience outside of school. However, references to subject areas in curriculum come from a variety of places outside of school (not only from the professional community of the parent discipline) and these fragmented external references may have more to do with student understandings of a subject than do formal thinking and logical, sequential, written curriculum.

Although educators have often tried to filter out experiences that are not considered legitimate curriculum content, many levels of such influence are reflected in students' artistic production and their conceptions of art. For example, teachers and parents have tried to prevent children from copying images from each other and popular culture sources in the hopes of promoting creativity, individuality, and psychological health. However, children's spontaneous drawings rely on graphic sources ranging from media images, comic books, and other popular sources, to other children's drawings (e.g., Duncum, 1984; Kindler, 1994; Wilson & Wilson, 1977). Students' attitudes and beliefs about art, including their misconceptions, exist all around them and are dependent, in part, on the many contradictions about art that pervade industrialized cultures. Social contradictions are reflected in student art as well (e.g., Duncum, 1989; Freedman, 2000) and should be considered in curriculum planning.

Issues concerning interpretations of seductive and widely distributed imagery are important to study today. Magazines, fine art, television, and other representations of identity, including the historical roots of contemporary visual culture, must be interrogated in classrooms, in part so that students become aware of the power of imagery and of their power as artists. Even university students rarely have a good understanding of the fabrication of images through computerization; they do not understand how the architects of beauty work to fashion our visions of our bodies or the intensely personal character of the relationship that has come to exist between these artists and their audience.

School practice continues to resist bringing the most powerful and seductive qualities of visual culture into classrooms. Instead of making these qualities transparent, curriculum is often designed in ways that actually mystify and hide these qualities because considerations of art in classrooms have often been intended to control, manage, and objectify, rather than reveal the social, cultural, and personal interactions and influences of visual culture. Part of the mystification of visual culture in school has been a separation of image from text and a valuing of text over image. In part, it is the separation of art-making from text-making in school that has been a critical reason for the particular conceptual location of art in school. In contrast to text-based curriculum, art curriculum depends on images of beauty and other sensual content. Education about the sensual qualities that promote perceptual pleasure in order to inform, seduce, convince, and so on, diminish in importance in school, in part precisely because they are pleasurable. School is not conceptualized as a pleasurable place and the common use of metaphors of science (e.g., "cold, hard facts") as models for education contrast strongly with the arts as a foundation for intellectual growth.

The field of art education has, of course, been influenced by views about what is appropriate to show to children and to allow students to make. Determinations of appropriateness often illustrate the fear that adults have of the power of the visual arts. Such fears extend from fine art to the mass media and are not altogether unfounded. Even television channel selection reflects identity and works in ways that construct identity. For students who spend much of their time watching television and who are looking for role models, their choices are highly potent for defining ways in which students look, act, and think. Students look to images as advance organizers—visual culture shapes the way they read texts, create themselves, and look at the world.

Educators are challenged to bring objects and images into class for analysis in ways that may not be typically seen in school. This can be done at the request of students, as was the case when I was invited to be on a panel at a local high school organized by an art teacher whose students were curious about the differences between art and pornography. The panel also included an art historian, an artist, and a lawyer. The discussion was informative (and occasionally embarrassing) but clarified to the students that the line between art and pornography was blurry even for adults. The discussion also helped students to understand that definitions emerged in the context of institutions and broad social categories (legal, commercial, religious, and so on), illustrating the importance of these in making distinctions concerning the visual arts.

Because appropriate curriculum content is sometimes based on the idea of promoting consensus, educators are often concerned that conflict in curriculum will only confuse students, and teachers are careful not to teach about professional conflicts in school (Graff, 1987). However, if we want education to be intellectually challenging, educators must take the responsibility to teach about conflicts because conflicts often give rise to meaning. If cultural institutions in a democracy are to educate enlightened citizens who take part in political decision-making and work together to improve cultural conditions, then relationships and conflicts of meaning in the realm of images must be considered in curriculum.

Cultural Fragments in Curriculum

In order to challenge the ways in which art is commonly depicted and taught in schools, and to suggest more equitable and enriching ways of teaching and thinking about visual culture, we must consider the ways in which cultural knowledge is shaped by curriculum and instruction. In the past, much of the discussion about diversity and reform in art education has focused on change in teaching practices. One view is that teachers should simply supplement published or unpublished curriculums, largely built on models of the disciplines of Western fine art, with multicultural content. Stuhr (1991, 1994) has equated this activity with the first level of Sleeter and Grant's (1987) multicultural approaches to education. This simple, supplementary approach to art education is due, in part, to the ways in which government and school district officials have responded to demands for equitable schooling. Their attempts at multiculturalism have often been couched in terms of fair "distribution" or "treatment," suggesting that what is needed is a certain number of lessons about a particular culture or a special (perhaps therapeutic) set of activities where women and men of color are included. In classrooms, such legislation can become reduced to a requirement that lessons contain a specified number of artifacts made by people of certain cultures.

The ideal purposes of including culturally diverse art in curriculum is to promote an understanding of the richness of visual culture, increase acceptance of disenfranchised groups, help students learn about relationships between traditional and contemporary art forms, and inform students about the aesthetic contributions of world cultures. However, published art curricula (which should be exemplars) do not always contextualize even Western art and often disassociate art from its multicultural contexts, basing analysis on modernist models of epistemology and aesthetics. The use of these models and quota systems result in inappropriate juxtapositions of culture, often misinforming students and further disenfranchising the groups that curriculum is meant to include. This occurs, in part, because the *technical* and *formalistic* attributes of artifacts are often focused upon, making vitally different cultural artifacts appear to be similar. It also occurs because art is taught within a discourse of extreme individualism, without attention to the ethnocentrism of this idea.

The problem is exacerbated by the use of published curriculum texts that are now out of date. For example, a second grade art textbook that was written in the late 1980s, but is still used by many districts in the United States, has a picture of a Navaho woman weaving on a loom and is juxtaposed with a closeup photograph of the woven plastic strips of a lawn chair that might be found at a local department store (Chapman, 1987). Rather than addressing the important differences in function, design, and production reflected in these images, the text highlights the relatively less important similarities in the physical structure of "woven" objects. To update the use of this text, a better comparison might be between the Navaho image and a picture of the conceptual work of art titled *Powwow Chair* by artist Edgar Heap of Birds which consists of a lawn chair placed on a box of dirt taken from the reservation where the artist resides. According to the artist, this piece was produced in response to questions he has been asked that refer to stereotypes, such as whether Native Americans really sit cross-legged during powwows.

In another example, a published curriculum contains a slide of two Northwest Coast Indian totem poles showing one in the background and a part of another in the foreground (Alexander, 1988). In this picture, the photographer has shown what is important in Western aesthetics: the pole in the background is so distant that the form as a whole can be seen and, in the foreground, an individual face carved into the other pole is shown in closeup as if it were a portrait (a Western art form). In neither pole are we able to see the interrelationship of figures as one meets another, which is an important visual and spiritual aspect of the totem. Curriculums are filled with such juxtapositions that reflect a reconstitution of culture as mainstream Western aesthetic theory is drawn upon for interpretation and analysis.

Appropriately addressing issues of visual culture in school requires an understanding of the daily visual experiences of students. That means that curriculum must keep up with changes in the visual world. This is difficult to do if teachers and teacher educators do not have time to become acquainted with, for example, the types of websites students tend to visit or the films they go to see.

Problems concerning teaching culture in education are usually assumed to be located in occurrences that take place in a classroom, rather than to be inherent in the structure of schooling (Sleeter & Grant, 1987). The interests of teaching art forms of different cultures often conflict with other interests of schooling. As a result, the complexity of teaching about diversity or any other social issue connected to visual culture, such as ecology, cannot be handled by individual teachers or solely on the level of written curriculum. Multicultural and cross-cultural perspectives of art education demand a deeper understanding by all those concerned with schooling, as well as the general public. The character of instruction and institutional boundaries of schooling, even aspects of schooling that seem neutral, such as scheduling, must be reconsidered if such an understanding is to be reached.

Daily, and from a variety of sources, students get mixed messages and fragmentary information about the visual arts, many of which include stereotypes or present art as historically static. Clear messages about particular contexts are important if students are to understand the multiple meanings of visual culture. These messages can maintain the integrity of difference, yet attend to global concerns. Clear messages about culture are extremely complex, in part because thinking of cultures as separate has become increasingly difficult. Anthropologist James Clifford's (1988) phrase "ethnographic surrealism" represents the ways in which anthropologists work at combining fragments of various cultures in a conceptual collage, where bits of beliefs, activities, and so on that did not originate together are brought into a common space to provide new meaning as a whole. However, while cultures interact, maintaining the notion of different artistic traditions in historically separate cultures can be important for the sake of identity. In part, identity is defined by such traditions. Therefore, in school, students should study art both as a reflection of particular histories and as a result of bridged histories. Curriculum can include when, where, and how cultural connections can be made between various forms of visual culture and the relationship of these connections to social and cultural transformation.

CONCLUSION

Change in art education can promote the transformation of cultural representations in school at large (e.g., Lanier, 1969; Neperud, 1988; Stuhr et al., 1992), and effectively help educators to meet democratic goals. A visual culture curriculum is a collage for learning that illuminates and demonstrates an awareness of the fragile and fragmentary state of much contemporary cultural knowledge, as well as the resilience of cultural traditions. Teaching such a curriculum includes providing for students an introduction to the characteristics and contexts of imagery and objects made by and for diverse groups of people, analytical critiques of the power of imagery and meanings of visual messages, and an opportunity to produce students' own contributions to visual culture. Teaching visual culture requires that art education be seen as fundamental to any study of culture and that culture is seen as foundational to art education.

Students are active learners and construct individual meaning from experience, but some common meanings are constructed by children through the pervasive common experience of media. As a result, inquiry-based methods of instruction, such as associative questioning, are particularly appropriate for studying contemporary imagery. These methods provide students with opportunities for interpretation that necessarily leads them in an interactive, artistic investigation outside the work and outside themselves, to find the sociocultural sources of their associations. These methods improve learning because they increase the number of attachments of new information to old knowledge, thereby strengthening the persistence of new knowledge as it is constructed.

CHAPTER 7

Art.edu

Technological Images, Artifacts, and Communities

VISUAL TECHNOLOGIES HAVE ALWAYS HAD AN INFLUENCE
on other visual culture, often as new art media, but also through the
ways in which they have caused us to reconceptualize previous art. For
example, photography changed the way in which people looked at painting. As well as changing formal rules, such as suggesting the idea of
the "closeup" to painters, photography increased attention to the individual qualities of each painting. It changed the criteria of judgment to
uniqueness and the concept of an original to something novel and
visionary. In the late 20th century, the range of visual technologies increased and became an increasingly important part of visual culture,
expanding cultural experience. An education in visual culture must
include attention to the issues surrounding visual technologies.

TECHNOLOGY AS A PART OF VISUAL CULTURE

Visual technologies are based on visual aesthetics, the power of which
is seductive and didactic (Ewen, 1988). They are sensual; they attract
and make people want to look at them. Global visual technologies depend on aesthetic strategies that promote perceptual pleasure and teach
us how to get more pleasure from them. Through this aesthetic, visual
technologies are used in ways that suggest, as well as represent. Using
technology, ideas are easily referenced and presented in forms that audiences are meant to interpret personally, but through culturally influenced eyes. Visual technologies easily and quickly enable us to cross
conceptual borders, providing connections between people, places, objects, ideas, and even professional disciplines.

Although human beings have historically struggled to develop the capacity to reproduce reality, with the development of computer technology, that goal has been surpassed. Computerization enables a hyperreality that is, in a sense, more real than reality. At the same time, it has a fictional quality not in its distance from the real, but in its suggestion that it could become real. The fictions of technological imagery can collapse time and space, are recycled from other media, and enhance toward some view of perfection. The enhancement of reality in postmodern imagery makes it appear more exquisite, more sublime—one might say more intensely "aesthetic"—and presents art educators with new challenges.

Imagery that appears to be realistic always illustrates artistic selection, but through technological capabilities the selective process is less transparent. Although in the past, a degree of believability may have been suggested by documentary photography and live television broadcasts, the producers of even "reality" TV programs, such as shows like *Survivor*, carefully select the footage they show to promote excitement and a particular construction by the audience of the personality of each show member. The range and influence of the inherent manipulation of reality in and through visual culture supports Umberto Eco's proposition that a sign is anything that can be used to lie. In postmodern culture, the importance of original intentions, higher aims, and verity that were used to maintain distinctions between fine art, popular visual culture, and education in the past are in dispute.

Technological imagery blurs the boundaries between truth and fiction by acting as both. This imagery has become an important aspect of students' lived experience and as such is part of their reality. Some students discuss television shows as if they were real, believe images they see on the Internet and in advertisements, and base social interactions on computer games. At the same time, pervasive images of violence enabled by newer technologies desensitize them to reality. By living on the edge of fiction and reality, technological imagery reference and cross-reference student life inside and outside of visual culture. For example, although students would not confuse playing a computer game with their bodily movement through an architectural space, the interactive quality of computer games (which involves visual and even physical movement) reifies students' conceptual movement through virtual space.

Much technological imagery has a fictional (perhaps, science fictional) quality: the content of television and the web, or for that matter *any* visual art form, is not necessarily "true." And yet, technological imagery has a form and pervasiveness easily construed as truthful. Technological images blur the boundaries between types of visual culture, making them more a part of real existence. Visual culture plays a crucial role in boundary crossing precisely because images are often more believable than texts and newer technologies have accentuated this condition. This is one of the reasons that newscasters use film footage and other photographic forms to sensationalize the news, make it more convincing, and draw viewers' attention through the use of the intense drama that visual images can convey. (News programs have also "morphed" into forums for advertising and marketing through the use of technological imagery, not only in the increasing amount of time given to actual commercials, but also through parts of the so-called news, such as movie criticism, events announcements, and spotlight stories on certain businesses and industries.) As David Morley (1992) points out, television newscasting now makes going outside frightening, so people stay in and watch TV. These functions of visual technologies are discussed in the following sections through examples.

Where Do Kids See Art?: The Aesthetics of Computer Gaming

The imagery in computer games will continue to become increasingly sophisticated. This sophistication is, in part, to attract student users. Computer game company personnel know that interesting and conceptually complex imagery is seductive. Internet multiplayer game services, such as Heat.net, Dwango, MPlayer, Kali, Ten, or Engage, or sites such as the Internet Gaming Zone or the Red Orb Zone, provide forums for play with complex simulations. Such games allow students to role-play fantasy through visual arts forms. Many of these games have sophisticated graphics and high levels of complexity in their imagery, music, and stories. Often such games simulate violence and are tailored for boys, but some have been designed with girls in mind.

In contrast to action, combat, or sports games, which tend toward violence; adventure games such as Myst, which was released in 1993; and its sequel Riven depend on problem solving and basic knowledge of art and science. Myst and Riven are produced by Red Orb Entertainment whose parent company, Broderbund, has a long (relative to any software development) record of producing educational software. Broderbund was started by entrepreneur Doug Carlson who is said to have coined the term *edu-tainment* when talking about his computer games (Broderbund was purchased by the Learning Company).

At 5 million copies sold, Myst is the best-selling CD-ROM game. Riven, which is more dynamically interactive, was released in the 1998 and has sold over 1 million copies. Clearly, these two computer games have been viewed and used by hundreds of thousands of students. This in itself is a good reason to include them when considering issues of visual culture. However, the processes of production, visual character-istics, content, and processes of use involved in such games make con-sideration of their educational influences even more compelling. These computer games exemplify the border crossing between visual forms of entertainment and education. They are problem-solving simulations, entertaining games, and examples of computer art.

The process of producing Riven involved recycling ideas through, for example, the work of an animator who moved from Disney to the Cyan development team to work on the software and a trip to Santa Fe to take photographs of adobe and other textures to be mapped onto the geometric structures of graphic objects such as buildings. It also involved live action actors, thereby combining movie effects with computer game interaction.

The particularly interesting aspect of these games is that they are all graphic. Although the story is about writing books that transport people, including the players, to other worlds, the primary means through which one gets information is visual. The visual effects are seductive indeed. Such games can seem addictive and players can be drawn into them so much so that they think about the visual effects and try to solve the problems even when they are away from the screen. When doing research for this book, I began playing these games and found myself even dreaming about the imagery. To deny the power of such rich visual culture would be foolhardy.

The response to such computer games is similar to that of film, video, and television. As discussed at greater length below, some tele-vision programs are now primarily visual shows, with very little dia-logue, and students buy videos that are all computer graphics with no words for entertainment. In such videos, a story is implied in the graphic sequences, but the story is left open to suggestion. Rock videos are some-times less about the music than about visual effects used to quickly and efficiently convey suggestions of sex, violence, and other concepts that make us want to look.

True, such games are eye candy, but are also powerful because they draw players into another, more seductive world through visual imag-ery. One can easily lose all track of time in the same way one does when creating a work of art. When creating a work of art, we are drawn in-side ourselves through processes of creating and interact with images, people, places, and stories inside our heads. When viewing art, playing a computer game, or watching a film, we engage with the creators as we seek to understand their creation while we create our own images and stories at their suggestion. Interacting with a visually complex computer game can be a powerful experience because it is suggestive of many possible stories and new images that spin away from the screen the player sees.

Perhaps this is the reason that people, particularly children and adolescents, can play the same computer games and watch the same films, videos, and television programs over and over. Although older research on student television viewing indicates that students do not reflect on their viewing while in front of a TV that controls their viewing pace (in contrast to books that are read at a reader's own pace) I have often heard students reflect on films at great length after viewing. They may not necessarily reflect on the things adults would wish, but thoughts are expressed, alternative scenarios developed, characters discussed, and so on. Recent research on television viewing confirms that students tend to watch intermittently, going away from the screen, paying attention to other things, talking with other viewers, and other activities that take them away from the story. During these times, they may be reflecting on alternative story lines, predicting what will happen next, or solving a mystery. As a result, they may develop many stories for a single program and hence will be able to watch it many times without getting bored.

Computer games promote certain types of learning. I have interviewed gamers on chat sites who have told me that aspects of learning are what make games interesting. For example, I asked a gamer using the name Heroman, "What makes a game addictive?" Heroman's response was,

> the phrase "easy to learn, impossible to master" comes to mind . . . a small learning curve makes the game more fun, however a large learning curve allows for the game to bring the user farther in.

Such games promote the development of many alternative answers to questions and various routes to establish a narrative. This is in contrast to the way in which a book or traditional film is structured, but even the feature film industry has begun to produce films that are less linear (one might say, more postmodern) in their storytelling. Films such as *Brazil, Being John Malkovitch*, and *Run Lola Run* illustrate some of these changes. *Brazil*, one of the earliest postmodern feature-length films (a project of Monty Python member Terry Gilliam) expanded and collapsed time and space, taking characters through a nonlinear story with complex visual effects. *Being John Malkovitch* was loosely constructed around ideas about what might happen when people take up residence inside other people's minds. The visual effects of this film include Malkovitch's encounter with a room full of duplicates of himself. In *Run Lola Run*, the film was cut and pasted in various ways to show different sequences going on at the same time. With the development of digital video cameras, both students and professionals can produce "films."

The Truth about Art Is Its Fictional Quality: The Example of *The Blair Witch Project*

The Blair Witch Project is a good example of the way in which the relationships between the various forms of visual culture that students spend the most time with have changed the forms themselves. *The Blair Witch Project* was originally the idea of two filmmaking students at Florida State University. When they approached their teacher with the idea in 1992, she scoffed at it, and yet it has become one of the most interesting media phenomena since Orson Welles's radio spoof on a "news flash" about visitors from another planet. The film is a fake documentary about three students who disappeared when they were in search of the Blair witch story, a mythology that was created by the filmmakers. It was produced for a reported $30,000 and made $48 million in its first week.

The premise of the film is that it shows the tapes that were found several years after the students' disappearance. The form of the film is mainly shaky video camcorder footage of the three actors in the woods. The actors were not stars and ad lib most of the script. In order to lend credibility to the actors' performance, the directors left the three out in the woods for a week camping with little food, and scared them occasionally by shaking bushes and making eerie sounds. Tired and hungry, the actors convincingly played terrified researchers who were at each other's throats by the end of the film. After several screenings and trips back to the editing room to cut some of the shakiest bits, the filmmakers took it to the Sundance Festival to try to find a distributor. Although most of the Hollywood producers had the same reaction as the directors' teacher, it got picked up by people who knew how to make it a hit via the website that the directors had launched in 1998. The website already had a small following and the distributor further developed the idea with new fake news clips, interviews, and outtakes from the original film footage each week in order to create the legend and make the missing persons story seem real. They also plastered college campuses with flyers about the "missing students" just prior to the end of the school year before the summer release of the film, so that the students would go off to their homes in different parts of the country and start talking about the story.

The buzz worked. Visits to the website grew before the film was released. By the time the film came out a loyal audience had already been formed, reversing the previously common development of a film website after release, helping to maintain interest until a sequel is released. Critics supported the tenacity of the independent filmmakers in their use of the Internet, but as one critic stated,

> The real key, though, remains the film. Unlike recent horror hits like *Scream*, it avoids irony and self-reference, which distances viewers; instead its porous surfaces draw them in . . . Though the jumpy style has alienated some older viewers, it taps a generational linguistic trope, one more fundamental than the latest slang. To Gen-X and -Y audience raised on handheld TV programs like "Cops" and MTV's "The Real World," deliberately low-fi recordings of groups like Pavement or the Wu-Tang Clan, and the funky misspellings of Internet newsgroups, grainy equals real, immediate. Wholly created by the production process, the jerk of a video camera or the crackle of a scratchy vinyl record has come to stand for the truer reality behind the process. (Leland, 1999, p. 49)

Of course, *The Blair Witch Project* is not the first film to come from behind and make a financial killing, but it may have been the first to illustrate ways in which students can shape the media by crossing over high and low tech boundaries and by suggesting the possibility that increasing the already extreme violence of filmmaking may not be the only option for the future. As Daniel Myrick (who codirected the film with Eduardo Sanchez) states: "Every now and then, art, whatever its form, gets back down to its roots" (quoted in Leland, 1999).

STUDENT USES OF ART AND TECHNOLOGY

Most educators understand that the only way to effectively teach is to start where the students are conceptually located. In the case of teaching about the visual arts, this means giving attention to the ways in which students engage with a range of mass media, computer games, rock videos, and so on. Students often repeat mottoes, create categories, and make generalizations about the arts before understanding the complexity of their related concepts. This is common in many areas of learning. As psychologists Gelman, Coley, and Gottfried (1994) state, "Classifications that appear theory-based are not always a direct consequence of theories. Specifically, people (especially children) may sometimes learn the 'theory-based' classification before they learn the theory" (p. 343).

People involved in the entertainment industry, including those who make interactive products such as software developers who make computer games "are so worried about losing their audience's attention that they feel they must continually bombard it with new experiences . . . Reflective mode must seem frightening to these people" (Norman, 1993, p. 218). Promoting many different ways to achieve this reflection mode is an important purpose of art education and one of the reasons that teaching visual culture has become so important. Even young children, such as the boy in Figure 7.1, become immersed in visual culture collections.

The social conditions of viewing are vital to the way in which visual messages are received and understood (Morley, 1992). The process is a highly interactive relationship between imagery and audience in which cultural and personal meanings are created. Both cultural and personal meanings are created as a result of social knowledge, including, for example, gendered associations, formal and informal education, and socioeconomic level. Therefore, focusing only on the technical aspects of visual arts, such as manipulating computer software or animating film, in curriculum may result in the loss of a vital aspect of imagery in students' lives.

However, students not only respond to visual culture; they take part in the creation of it, including through their influence on culture industries. For example, fads can start among children as easily as among advertising agents and companies that sell soft drinks and sport shoes. Marketers spend millions of dollars each year to find out from focus groups of kids what the next cool thing is. The influence of Pokémon was grossly underestimated by the industry and, although a few toys such as Barbie seem never to go out of style, millions of dollars were spent on *Star Wars* marketing and product development in 1999 for the new films, but most children just did not buy it. Even the Disney corporation, which has had success in the film-to-toy trade, has also had some major failures in their attempts to predict children's tastes.

Students at every level of education have the capacity to take part in the production of visual culture through their artistic uses of technology. Newer technologies are visual art media in their potential to enable the production of things never before seen. Often students at the high school and higher education levels initiate their own uses of technology to make a range of visual culture forms, from researching and

Figure 7.1. Child and his *Star Wars* collection.

Photos: Jennifer Trueman   (a)

(b)

(c)

creating their own costumes for long action role plays to making their own rock videos to developing their own websites to display and critique their artistic work and the work of other students on a global scale. The scope of student artistic production at all ages reveals broad interest in and increasing knowledge of technological media.

PRODUCING ON SCREEN

Artistic production with computers is an important student use of technology. The social aspects of this production include a concern about students becoming isolated and antisocial as a result of sitting in front of a screen. However, classroom research has demonstrated that students of various ages actually may work best in groups when using computers in school (e.g., Johnson, Johnson, & Stanne, 1986; Rysavy & Sales, 1991). This conclusion has been reported based on studies of a range of computer uses, from databases (Ehman, Glenn, Johnson, & White, 1992) to computer graphics (Freedman, 1989), and involves a range of collaboration types, from pairs of students working at the same computer to students who correspond by electronic mail.

One of the uses of computer technology in art classrooms is the generation of interactive graphics with paint programs, video capture, animation software, multimedia systems, etc. When students create computer graphics, they often find that the most stimulating aspect of their work is the "trial and error" capacity of the technology, including the capacity for seriation, which is the process of producing a series of images based on a single image (Freedman 1989, 1991). Students can test colors, move shapes around, animate objects, and recycle pictures quickly and easily without making permanent changes to an original image. This enables students to interact with each other's work in ways that are unlike traditional media because changes can be made in images as a result of critique without changing the original image.

Computer networks also provide powerful possibilities for student learning. The interactive capabilities of computer technology coupled with the vast amount of imagery and information available on the Internet give students a wide range of resources that they can download, print out, cut and paste into their own files, and so on. Several virtual exhibitions of student art have already been established on the Internet. The net can even make it easy for students to communicate with each other from different locations. Through the use of home pages and E-mail, groups and individuals can instantly communicate with other groups at long distance, enabling students to work together who would otherwise have little opportunity for contact. Students with common interests can "get in touch" with each other and students who have little in common can learn about each other.

Equity issues, such as whether students (and which students) have access to computers, demand attention if we are to understand student uses of technology. Unfortunately, at times computers actually support the inequities of schooling (DeVillar & Faltis, 1991; Muffoletto & Knupfer, 1993). A growing body of literature indicates that gender differences exist in computer use (e.g., Canada & Brusca, 1991; Diem, 1986; Freedman, 1989). Students with different ethnic backgrounds may also have different experiences with technology (DeVillar & Faltis, 1991; Freedman & Liu, 1996). For example, one study I did with a colleague indicated that students of different ethnic backgrounds had different attitudes about and knowledge of computers, had different cross-cultural communication patterns, and used different learning processes when working with computers (Freedman & Liu, 1996).

WATCHING ART: STUDENTS AS AUDIENCE

Even in classrooms where students do not have access to computer technology for production, they can learn how to analyze images created through the use of advanced technology. Many of the images students see every day have been created or manipulated using computer technology and other advanced technological media. Analyses of these imagery and the ways in which the images are produced can help students understand the artistic possibilities of visual technologies and the pervasiveness of their use and influence.

Visual technologies reference fragmented and often contradictory multidisciplinary and intercultural knowledge, which may have more to do with student understanding of a school subject than does a curriculum based on the structure of a discipline. Such postmodern visual experience cannot be effectively translated in a traditional curriculum framework. Thus, the role of teachers and students as active viewers will change as we increasingly interact with technological images. As a result of increased interactions with visual technologies and other popular visual culture, students need increased critical guidance that teachers can provide. This does not mean teachers should act merely as facilitators. Rather, it means that teachers will have to increase attention to the interpretive and critical analysis of imagery and other visual forms of information. In the following sections, I discuss some of the topics of a visual culture curriculum that includes analyses of technological imagery.

Visualizing Computer Graphics

Any curriculum that focuses on visual technologies should include a consideration of the aesthetic peculiarities of computer graphics and mass media imagery. Elements and principles of design are apparent in computer graphics and have antecedents in the fine arts. However, they are often used somewhat differently when computers are involved. Light is emitted as well as reflected, simulation has become what Baudrillard has called a hyper-reality, interaction involves physically changing a work of art, and movement is at breakneck speed. Animation principles, such as point of view, are also important to the study of computer graphics.

When using computers to produce art, aesthetic questions arise, such as, What is the work of art? Is there an art object? If so, is it conceptual in the sense that it no longer exists when it leaves the screen? Who is the artist(s)? What part do the software designers play? How should computer graphic art be displayed? Is it appropriate for one person to change another person's work? The formulation of and debate about such questions is an important aspect of teaching about technology-based images.

As well as the aesthetic qualities of computer graphics, the history of computer graphics could be included in curriculum. This history includes the emergence of graphics as a result of national defense interests. In the United States several early developments were sponsored by the federal government, through agencies like NASA, which sought to visualize, animate, and enhance images of outer space. However, artists soon realized the possibilities of computer graphics for other purposes and began to use art concepts to produce increasingly sophisticated images. Commercial uses of computer graphics also began early, but were not commonly seen in feature-length films and advertising until the 1980s.

The subject matter in computer graphics is also an important topic for curriculum. For example, much of the professional work in computer animation is currently produced as science fiction, which blurs the boundary between art and science. The unstable and border-crossing tendencies of computer graphics often give them a postmodern flavor.

Computerized Images That Teach

Any single image can be interpreted in many ways, and some image makers, such as fine artists, have long deliberately constructed images that suggest unlimited and unstable meanings. In contrast, other image makers, such as advertisers, have typically produced images that they hope a particular audience will read in a "preferred" or "dominant" manner (Morley, 1992). For example, ads have generally been produced to represent certain possibilities for interpretation and not others in order to convince people to think and behave in a particular way. Recently, however, ad images have become increasingly manipulated through the use of computers. Advertisers have begun to shift from using subtle message techniques to using images to send messages in overt, even shocking ways, just as fine artists have done historically to grab an audience (Giroux, 1994). Also, advertisers have made deliberately complex images that suggest multiple, confusing, and even conflicting meanings to capture viewers' attention.

As a result, computers have destroyed any idea of photography as documentary evidence. They collapse time and space, creating virtual realities. What we see on a television screen as a stage set may be created entirely within a computer, and live action in different parts of the world can be seen simultaneously on the same screen. Most fashion magazine advertisements are now touched up through the use of computers. Wrinkles and blemishes are erased, makeup is enhanced, noses are narrowed, eyes made larger, jewelry is omitted, backgrounds are created, and even skin color is changed. Manipulated images have become so common in this context that untouched photographs are used to shock people into paying attention.

In the United States, such imagery works against European-American girls even more than other girls. In part, this is the case because European-American models are most often used in fashion photography. White girls see models of their own race as role models and think that it must be possible to look like them although, in fact, their appearance is only possible for a very small percentage of the population and for a very short time in their life. Research suggests that African-American girls tend to have better body images than European-American girls, in part, because they do not continually see unrealistic body images of their own race in magazines, on television, and so on. In one research project, African-American and European-American girls equally compared themselves and their friends to television images, had a drive to be thin, were dissatisfied with their bodies, and engaged in eating-disordered behaviors. However, the European-American girls chose a thinner ideal figure size than the African-American girls (Botta, 2000).

Although computers have certainly influenced the production and availability of idealized images, it is important to keep in mind that they have not caused the creation of the ideals. The manipulation of images of women by computer continues the long fine art tradition of representing gendered ideals. Consider Ingres's translation of female skin as a silk-sheeted bed in his *Odalisque* or the skin of Degas's nudes as a surface complex as a landscape. Such traditions tie various types of visual culture together.

However, computer capabilities do provide opportunities for image manipulation that traditional art media do not. For example, computers can enable the creation of virtual beings that look real. This example leads to questions that should be dealt with in school: Does this type of technological manipulation hurt women's and girls' images of themselves? Should any images of women in magazines be considered "real"? What does the mass distribution of images suggest about beauty and other aspects of aesthetics in the culture of advanced democracies?

The educational implications of these technological innovations derive, in part, from the use of popular culture images by students. Beach and Freedman's (1992) study of adolescents' interpretation of advertising images containing representations of gender demonstrated that students often place themselves in the fictional world of ads and use it as standards against which to judge reality. Their use of gender stereotypes based on ad images in this study was inconsistent with the equity goals of schooling. Technological images can teach students how to "read" them in ways that their creators intend. However, alternative, critical "readings" are possible if students are taught specifically how to critically analyze images. Through a contextual curriculum, students gain an awareness of the place of technology in the production and reproduction of, for example, visual stereotypes, and become aware of the perils and possibilities of the virtual world.

TELEVISION: THE NATIONAL CURRICULUM

The technological developments that enable and support mass communication have increased the availability of visual representations of all sorts to anyone who has access to television, computers, film, and other mass media. Visual forms of culture have become more accessible than literary forms. Approximately one third of the early adolescents in the United States watch five or more hours of television a day. People in the United States have more televisions and video recorders and spend more on advertising per capita than any other nation. More children watch a nationally broadcast television program than are taught from the same written school curriculum. In a sense, television has become the national curriculum and the media now provide edu-tainment.

The production of visual arts through the use of technology has become a critical issue in American art education. Through telecommunications, students learn *from the visual arts* a virtual curriculum over which no one person or group has control. Contemporary television disseminates images that are highly seductive and involve sophisticated aesthetics. More than any other technology, television illustrates the critical connections between images in advertising, fictional stories, comedy, drama, news broadcasting, documentaries, information on the web, film and video, and even outer space. On television, students see visuals from various cultures recycled in fine art, advertising, and other forms of visual culture. Soon, the television/web connection will be seen in households as often as TV. Television channels and programs have set up websites that have additional information related to a show and these contain references to other sites.

Students also learn *about the visual arts* through TV. They learn that art has the power to convince, persuade, seduce, make what is fiction seem to be fact, and to make reality appear unreal. The truth about fiction on television is that its images can collapse time and space, may be recycled from other media, and are enhanced toward some view of perfection. These representations of reality, are more intensely "aesthetic" than those of the past, and present art educators with new issues and problems. When television was new, people became concerned that students would have difficulty understanding its fictional quality; now, however, its fictional quality has become reality—that is, it is part of the lived experience of students' daily life.

Children's Television

In 1996, the U.S. Federal Communications Commission required that broadcast television channels (not cable channels) provide at least 3 hours of educational programming for children and adolescents each week. Although this act appears to have helped improve students' television viewing options, it has also resulted in an approval process dependent on exaggerated written claims that do not represent the actual, visual forms of the television programs. Television stations developed educational arguments for programs that most professional educators would not consider educational.

Research on children's television viewing behaviors indicate that children's interpretations of programming is what is important and that what might be good intentions of directors or producers are not as influential as adults might like to think. Several studies of children's view-

ing habits have revealed that few young children watch an entire program all the way through (Kearney, 1988). Instead they go in and out of
the room, pay attention to other things, have conversation and so on.
And British research indicates that children usually tend to prefer adult
programs over those designed for children (Blumler, 1992).

The sheer amount of time that children spend viewing television
suggests a profound impact of the medium. As Furnham and Stacey
(1991) report:

> Purposive television viewing begins as early as the third year of life, though
> infants are exposed to television before then. At any age the average child
> or adolescent will spend more time watching television than in a school
> class, because most young people spend more than twenty hours per week
> watching television throughout the year. (p. 104)

The pervasiveness of television makes its fiction particularly influential. Distinctions between television fiction and reality may not be made
until the second decade of life because children have little firsthand experience with the world.

For example, literally thousands of studies have demonstrated that
children and adolescents who watch violence on television act out vio-
lently. In videotaped studies where young children watch cartoons and
other children's shows that include aggressive behaviors, such as hit-
ting, punching, and kicking, children who are left on their own with
other children, or even toys, replay this behavior.

Many studies over many years have demonstrated that students
develop sexist and racist attitudes at least in part through the influence
of television (e.g., Durkin, 1985; Greenfield, 1984; Lichter & Lichter,
1988).

> The amount of time the young spend watching television tends to be
> positively related to the strength of their sex stereotypes. This finding may
> reflect what television does to the young or the greater attraction of tele-
> vision for the more strongly sex-stereotyped youngsters or an interactive
> relation between the two. (Furnham & Stacey, 1991, p. 104)

TV and Postmodern Aesthetics

References to the visual arts, even those in school curriculum, come
from a variety of places outside as well as inside the professional arts
community. These fragmented external references influence student understanding of many aspects of life, from social relationships to the physics of the universe. As a result, the relationships between images, and

their interdisciplinary connections, including the sociopolitical conditions under which they are produced and seen, are vital to understanding fine art and other forms of visual culture.

Historically, television played a part in the separation of fine art from commercial art (Bogart, 1995). Although television was seen in its early days as a grand experiment in aesthetics, and broadcasters commissioned fine art painters, such as Ben Shahn, for advertising, background images, and so on, television helped to focus attention on the photographic image. It began to replace periodicals that were read for escape and which included fantasy art (Bogart, 1956). Advertisers increased their use of photography to be consistent with the imagery used in nonfiction media (Bogart, 1995). Also, television provided a vehicle for promoting recreational art production. For example, NBC ran the series *You Are an Artist* (later *Draw with Me* and *Learn to Draw*) for 25 years starting in 1946. In the series, commercial artist John Gnagy taught casual painters. However, not all art educators were happy about this innovative use of the technology. As art historian Michele Bogart (1995) reports:

> A committee of art educators headed by Museum of Modern Art education director Victor d'Amico protested to the network that the program stifled creativity and perpetuated "outmoded and authoritarian concepts of education" (p. 296).

Recreational art made the growing divisions between the visual arts even more apparent as promoters of modernism, such as Clement Greenberg, sought to narrow the definition of fine art.

Now, however, little criticism of the fine art content of television programming comes from members of the art community. Programs about art are usually seen on the Public Broadcasting Station channels or on the cable station Arts and Entertainment (another example of the collapse of these categories). Most are thoughtfully produced, but even if they were not, many people believe that any art on TV is publicity for the arts and that bad publicity is better than no publicity in a fame-focused environment. Rather, it is the influence of TV aesthetics that is at issue in making any televised program or commercial a mass-distributed part of the visual arts.

The good news is that students are now beginning to become sophisticated enough to understand the impact of television on their choices, values, and identities. In a *TV Guide* interview with a focus group of high school students, one boy said in response to a question about which television performer would be the next heartthrob, "I don't know; cute girls are so common. It's starting to become a bore, because they all look alike. The dudes, too" (Littlejohn, 1999, p. 32).

CONCLUSION

An influential interpretation of democracy in contemporary American education has been the acceptance of diversity and promotion of empowerment on all levels. Visual technologies represent democratic thought to many people because they are not yet controlled by a small group of individuals or a few companies. However, from an educational standpoint, such technological freedom has its problems. For example, students are now able to access all kinds of information through the Internet, without any assurance of quality.

This means that the roles and responsibilities of teachers and students who use these technologies for educational purposes must change. In contrast to the current pervasive conception of technology as an area of content, newer technological hardware and software should be thought of as media and infused into curriculum with other media. Teaching with and about visual technologies will need to be thought of as less a predetermined sequence of learning events and more as a creative, social process.

CHAPTER 8

Contributing to Visual Culture

Student Artistic Production and Assessment

INDIVIDUAL ARTISTIC PRODUCTION IS VITALLY IMPORTANT in the teaching of visual culture, but the studio in an educational setting is not one of a single artist alone. Rather, it is the foundation of a learning community and a socially interactive environment that involves individuals and groups in viewing, discussing, analyzing, debating, and making art. Visual culture is best understood when students are able to learn relationships between concepts and skills through their infusion in curriculum. Artistic production is a critical path to understanding, partly because the process and the product of art-making enables students to experience creative and critical connections between form, feeling, and knowing. It empowers students through their expression of ideas and construction of identities as it gives insight into the artistic motivations, intentions, and capabilities of others. As a result, any educational discussion of visual culture must include some consideration of the interaction between creating and assessing student art. In this chapter, the fusion of emotion and cognition are revisited from the perspective of student artistic production and assessment in social contexts.

Student artistic production is a visual illustration of the influence of the broad range of imagery and objects they encounter every day. Images are recycled in their art. Despite the fact that teachers have often tried to prevent children from copying, students' drawings rely heavily on graphic sources ranging from mass media images to other student art (e.g., see Duncum, 1988, for a review; Wilson, Hurwitz, & Wilson, 1987; Wilson & Wilson, 1977).

Students make visual art not merely for its formal, technical, or even private value; they do not only seek to improve their skills of representation or develop their own style. Students want to communicate and be understood, often about social issues. Although students' experiences may be private, their method of responding through art is public and the message is often communal. Through their art, students can express concerns, ask questions, interpret imagery, and make judgments. If education is working, students can make art that comments on social injustice, community change, and concern for the environment—issues about which they are often in the process of forming opinions. The primary purpose of such student art is not therapeutic; it is social and cultural. It is not just about individual emotions; it is about the personalization of social issues. The complexity of this perhaps subtle difference is critical if we intend to teach students about visual culture in relation to their world.

ASSESSMENT: FROM LIKING TO UNDERSTANDING

Part of the general functional rationality of modern art education is a scientific rhetoric that has provided the conceptual horizons for institutional reform discourses (Freedman, 1995). The Enlightenment project helped to shape contemporary ideas about the value and form of scientific thought in the development of all public systems. In the process of a general cultural rejection of the metaphysical from such systems, scientific rhetoric became increasingly important in the construction of answers to questions concerning curriculum and instruction.

Scientific rhetoric is not science per se. Rather, it is an element of certain professional discourses, including educational discourse, that exemplifies some common beliefs about the structure, applicability, and certainty of science. The rhetoric carries with it the assumption that social life may be systematically tested like the physical world. It is assumed that through testing, objective truths will be discovered and measured, or at least untruths will be revealed. It is further assumed that science progressively moves toward truth by achieving better methods, technologies, and data or by paradigmatic shifts that better provide a description of reality. Finally, scientific rhetoric is considered universally applicable, not only to the physical world it was intended to describe, but to the social world where it is used to prescribe.

Scientific rhetoric has been used in part to overcome conflict in educational settings. It suggests a "right" answer and therefore carries with it a resolution of educational debate. It does not carry with it a representation of the play of scientific ideas against a structural background of time and place. It does not, for example, represent science as involving a historically constructed ideology involving power relations influenced by politics, economics, and social struggles (Aronowitz, 1988). Rather, the rhetoric is considered neutral and self-contained, unattached to historical crises and social transformations. Yet the discourse itself is a historical representation.

Scientific conceptions of youth art have been critical to art education. Adults' conceptions of childhood have changed over the centuries and these changes have shaped educational purposes and practices (Aries, 1962). Children have been theoretically described as having certain "natures," and the theories have become prescriptions for appropriate upbringing in institutional settings and the home, legitimating and reifying the original beliefs.

Theories about the art of children have related to shifts in the social world. For example, in mainstream American culture, children's unsupervised drawings were generally ignored or ridiculed before the late 19th century. Even then, children were often prohibited from drawing in school except to copy adult art precisely. The classification of children's drawings as artistic expression only emerged at the end of the 19th century; yet, in the 20th century, children's drawings have been valued as an expression of psychological health to such an extent that adult artists have sought to recapture childlike qualities in their own work. Historically, such theories about children and child art have been applied in social settings, such as schools, and have fulfilled larger social purposes. Even when the purposes of art and art education appear to be individual, social agendas become visible as they are viewed within the contexts of cultures and institutions.

Nowhere is scientific rhetoric more clearly seen in art education than in assessment strategies. This is particularly the case at the K–12 public school level, where assessment in all school subjects is highly political and has become based on "educational standards" (which are usually stated as objectives rather than standards) and standardized testing.

Assessment Appropriate to Teaching Visual Culture

In a lead article in *Educational Researcher* published by the American Educational Research Association, Lorrie Shepard (2000) points to the importance of understanding the social and cultural conditions of assessment. Her focus is "not the kind of assessments used to give grades or to satisfy the accountability demands of an external authority, but rather the kind of assessment that can be used as a part of instruction to support and enhance learning" (4). Shepard acknowledges that social and cultural conditions have both positive and negative influences on learning and argues that educators must work to suppress, for example, the negative influences of high-stakes testing on students and teachers. Instead, she argues that assessment procedures should "include observations, clinical interviews, reflective journals, projects, demonstrations, collections of students' work, and students' self-evaluations" (p. 8).

These assessment procedures have long been common to the arts. Unfortunately, elementary and secondary art educators have begun to move away from these methods as pressure has increased for legitimating teaching and learning with testing. A cartoon in *The New Yorker* (January 15, 2001) of a couple seated in front of the desk of a school counselor who is saying, "Unfortunately, all evidence of your son's intelligence is purely anecdotal," illustrates the problem. The methods of assessment that arts communities have long used to promote quality are considered "anecdotal," subjective, and illegitimate outside the arts, while testing is considered scientific, objective, and therefore legitimate.

If we want students to appreciate the power and diversity of art, we must consider visual culture a basic part of human existence and accept that certain psychophysical responses are shared across individuals and communities. However, the communal value of any particular work of art is socially and culturally constructed. It emerges from conditions ranging from the politics of its production to its historical and contemporary meanings for a viewing audience. As a result, a broad range of experience with visual culture, including its production, will help people to shift from a "personal" like or dislike of art images or objects to understanding.

Students learn more about the complexities of assessing art when instructors model for them the ways in which serious artistic judgments are made. They are not made based solely on personal preference, but rather on community debate and consensus. Likewise, experienced teachers' assessments of student art are not merely personal; they are an expression of expert opinion based on education, including a large imagic store of student art examples against which any new example is judged. Assessment of art is not a matter of being "subjective" or "objective"; it is a matter of experience.

Even at the elementary level, formative and summative assessments are important to conduct when students are making art. Boughton (1994) describes these forms of assessment in the following way:

> In the course of a day, teachers provide feedback to students . . . used by students to gauge their progress and to make decisions about actions they

may need to make to assist in their learning, or the improvement of their studio products. The manner in which teachers provide this information may be very informational, as in incident comment, or more formal, as in structured interview or written report . . . such judgments are called formative assessments.

At the end of a major unit of study, [summative] judgements are usually made about students' overall performance to facilitate "gatekeeping" decisions such as "progress to the next level of study," or simply "pass or fail." . . . Formative feedback tends to be rich and descriptive, and is intended to provide a clear indication to students of the strengths and weaknesses of their work, whereas summative feedback is often expressed as a letter grade or numeral containing no clue about the quality of the work, but does indicate the students' standing in a normative sense. (pp. 5–6)

Art educators are experts who have developed imagic stores that they rely on to formatively assess student work. Rubrics, checklists, and other forms of textual and numerical assessment can be used in conjunction with this imagic store, or with physical benchmarks on small or large scales, to aid reliability in assessment, but the judgments are still always made based on instructors' visual experiences. Rubrics can be used to assess individual works of art or used in conjunction with portfolio assessment in order to assess the growth and development of student work over the course of a unit, a class, or several classes. Rubrics can result in a numerical score representing quality, but in art education, descriptions of level should be associated with a *visual equivalent.*

The assessment of student work can also involve oral and written documentation based on peer and self-assessment, critiques, and other forms of response (Boughton, 1996). Assessments should relate to the concepts and skills that students are intended to learn, but must also allow for those students who go beyond "the box" of instructional objects. Even assessment procedures should allow for this possibility through, for example, group critique. When teaching postmodern concepts and skills, such as suggestiveness, which demand multiple, varied, and extended responses, the teacher may not be the best respondent for determining the total success of the work. In such cases, student response through small group or large group discussions or written feedback may be effective in helping teachers judge whether a work is successful. Also, the form of student art may indicate alternative forms of assessment. For example, installations, performances, and community projects may be most effectively assessed through the inclusion of audience/community response.

Adolescents are often particularly interested in the suggestive, symbolic attributes of visual culture, which go beyond the formal qualities of the objects (Freedman, 1995). These students can become deeply involved in making and viewing, not necessarily because of formal qualities per se; but rather, through the ways in which possible meanings have been artistically presented and their personal and group extension of those meanings. As curriculum changes to attend to these student interests, changes in assessment are required. One of my graduate students illustrated this in her report on a new course she was developing:

> Both the written committee reviews and the large group discussions proved essential for assessing the success of the students' art product . . . Sometimes students drew associations between materials and images with which I had no experience. For example, two students constructed an assemblage based on their childhood memories. They brought in a wide selection of toys and games, glued and plastered them together in a somewhat random fashion, and attached working Christmas lights. The work was titled "Childhood Pinball Machine." At first glance, the work had little order to it. It was not unified, had no center of attention, and did not follow most of the formal "rules" of art. In contrast, two other students . . . constructed an assemblage based on a trip to Niagara Falls . . . [which] had a wonderful unity of color and texture and a Monet-esque painting of a waterfall. Initially, I regarded "Niagara Falls" to be the more successful assemblage. I, having been trained in a formalist tradition, responded to it using this lens. Yet, in the discussions and committee reviews of the artworks, the students had little to say about "Niagra Falls" and were overflowing with things to say about "Childhood Pinball Machine." They recalled all the times they have played with pogs, collected baseball cards, and played arcade games. They were excited about the addition of an old car headlight which reminded them of stadium lights . . . what I discovered from this discussion was that "Childhood Pinball Machine" was rife with associative power, while Niagara Falls was simply beautifully painted and carefully arranged. From a postmodern standpoint, then, "Childhood Pinball Machine" was a more successful artwork. (Pereira, 2000, p. 20)

Making "Alternatives" Standard

As reported by Castiglione in 1996, over 40 states were in the process of investigating forms of assessment, such as portfolio assessment, as alternatives to statewide testing. Portfolios, which have been used by art educators for centuries but are newly of interest to educators in other school subjects, are powerful structures for assessing student studio work and studio work created in conjunction with student writing and speaking about art. Portfolio assessment should not be a matter of assessing each individual work of art as much as a holistic assessment that can take into account the breadth and depth of student learning. Portfolios can involve one-on-one interactions between student and teacher in which an exploration of the relationship between the visual and textual work can be done to extend ideas and increase the complexity and sophistication of future work. Such assessment strategies can inform students about the process of critical thinking that is involved in making and assessing works of art.

Bringing into the classroom outside expert knowledge concerning the valuing of art, through, for example, guest speakers, professional critics' writings, and so on, is important, but experts often disagree and the people most knowledgeable about a work of art may not be members of the professional fine art community. Focusing on differences of opinion in the professional community can help students to see that multiple ways of looking at art can be justified and that we need not always look for a consensus of opinion. Local people who are knowledgeable about particular aspects of visual culture can be called upon to provide students with information and aid their understanding. A student's own cultural context can also provide important contributions to teaching and learning.

At an early age, students can begin to learn about the connections between art and social life, which is an important step toward understanding why a particular work of art, and art in general, is valued. At the elementary school level, children begin to learn distinctions, categories, and generalizations of many types and are able to discriminate among a variety of styles, subjects, forms, meanings, and purposes of visual culture. At this level, students can begin to understand why different individuals and cultural groups have made different visual representations of the same subject matter (such as people, animals, events, etc.) and grasp the value of this variety of representation. At the same time, comparing artifacts from different cultures must be done carefully, because what may be similar in appearance may be fundamentally different in purpose and meaning. By pointing out these differences, teachers can help students see that an understanding of art requires a search beyond the surface that can give students skills in investigation and help them to develop visual sensitivity.

CRITIQUE AND COMMUNITY

Students develop an awareness of quality in the visual arts early in life and this awareness can be enhanced through the development of critique capabilities. Among the difficulties instructors find with critique is that students are usually very concerned with being correct and the ways in which they are seen in the eyes of their peers. By adolescence, many students have a preference for realism in art and are often frustrated when they are unable to produce highly realistic images. These students can learn the production skills necessary for them to feel comfortable about producing their own imaginative work, as well as gaining an appreciation of their work and the work of others, by working in a safe environment for producing, writing, and talking about a range of visual culture.

Critical Making and Viewing

Because students are becoming increasingly aware of local and global social conditions, and are immersed in the culture of their peers, they should be encouraged to develop a critical awareness, including making critical statements through their own art. Culturally aware art educators (e.g., Blandy, 1994; Chalmers, 1981; Congdon, 1989; Stuhr et al., 1992; Wasson et al., 1990) recommend that these students use sociological and anthropological methods, such as interviewing artists and bringing artists from the community into the classroom to gain knowledge of visual culture contexts that can lay the groundwork for students making their own statements through artistic production. Students can draw on feminist and other sociocultural critique methods (e.g., Garber, 1990; Hicks, 1990) to respond to issues of identity in visual culture. Through these investigations, students develop an understanding of the ways in which social groups and cultural issues are visually represented and judged. These investigations should give attention to issues relevant to students as well as to adults and can be done with students as soon as they begin to attend to their social surroundings. In excellent elementary and middle-level school programs, I have seen even early adolescents do forms of cultural critique through their art, making comments, for example, on their fears of terrorism and war, makeup testing on animals, student bullying, skateboarding laws, and environmental concerns.

Critique of student art can promote inquiry into general issues of visual culture. This can be done individually or in a group, initiated by students or by the teacher, and done during or after production. Ongoing critique is part of any good art lesson and the types of critical analysis used in art education are useful methods for developing reflective general educational practice (Eisner, 1982, 1985; Schon, 1987). When students make artistic images and objects, they should articulate related concepts and skills, state reasons for their decisions, and explain what they believe to be successful or unsuccessful about the work.

Through in-class critique, educators can provide students with ways to consider, assess, and act that can help them to make positive changes in their work and make constructive ideas about visual culture. Student interaction during critique disperses control and responsibility in the classroom and promotes student interpretation as part of the construction of knowledge.

The critique processes used for student discussion of professional or other adult works of art can be used for their critique of art in class. As discussed above, critiques provide another modality for learning, just as music adds to the visual art of dance and dialogue to theater. Many forms of critique can be done to enhance learning and illustrate the point that knowledge in and through art is socially interactive. Group critique is often most effective in small groups and can be facilitated through the use of several different formats, each producing a somewhat different result.

Peer and Self-Assessment: Group Critique Methods

Group verbal critique usually involves an interactive discussion, focusing on a student(s)' production or performance, that includes the student artist(s), a group of student peers, and a teacher. This process can be carried out in large groups, small groups, or pairs and does not necessarily require a teacher to work continually with a group of students. For example, students can form small critique groups and then report on their discussion to the teacher or the class. Critiques can involve "scaffolding," which is a process that enables students to understand better than each would be able to alone. Palinscar and Brown (1984) developed a scaffolding procedure to improve student understanding of texts involving the following steps: students generate questions about a text they have just read, clarify what they do not understand, summarize what they have read, and develop predictions for the meaning of what they do not understand. At first, the teacher should carefully guide scaffolding, then allow students to ask each question that will aid students in reflecting and forming conceptual connections (Webb & Palinscar, 1996).

When done well, critique depends heavily on verbal contributions by the students whose work is being assessed. During this discussion, students are often expected to demonstrate that their initial intentions coincided with lesson goals, that they met those intentions (or explain why their intentions changed or were not met), and that they learned concepts and skills. Students are also expected to articulate relevant art knowledge (for example, analyze the formal qualities of the work or relate it to a historical art style) and reflect on its meaning.

Alternative forms of critique can be used to help students understand group processes of production and appreciation of the arts. These alternative methods of procedure put student groups at the center of art inquiry and assessment. The following are examples of group critique methods that can be used in classrooms.

TRADITIONAL CRITIQUE
1. The teacher leads discussion of student art by assessing the work and/or asking students provocative questions.
2. Questions are based on objectives of the lesson, focus on judgments of quality, and recommendations for improvement, and may be comparative.

This form of critique efficiently communicates information and is directly tied to the objectives of the lesson.

STUDENT QUESTIONING
1. Each student selects a number of his or her works of art to present to the class.
2. Each student develops a few questions to ask the class about his or her work.
3. The student viewers may also ask questions of the student artist.

This and other student-directed forms of critique enable students to engage in discussion based on what they consider important about their art.

INDIVIDUAL DIALOGUE
1. Each student keeps a journal/sketchbook over a period of time.
2. Each student discusses the journal with the teacher one-to-one, taking part in a dialogue about what is written and about the work that was produced at the time it was written.
3. In group critiques, students and teacher may refer to the dialogue and relate it to general growth.

This form of critique enables students and teacher to become more familiar with student intents, motivations, and thought processes.

SMALL GROUP CRITIQUE
1. The students coordinate the critique so they do not rely only on the teacher's expertise.
2. Students work together in small groups to critique the work of each member of the group.
3. Each group of students then reports to the class on what happened during the process of their group critique.

This form of critique helps students to develop an understanding that quality is discernible, but complex, and may be determined through discussion and disagreement.

PEER PAIRS
1. Students work in pairs on one work of art or trade work with each other.
2. Students carry on a dialogue about their work, cooperatively critiquing the work and making suggestions for improvement.
3. During and after the critique, studio work should be carried on with additional dialogue.

This and other forms of small group critiques help students to articulate more clearly about their work and the work of others.

ROLE PLAY
1. Students study or research comments made by art professionals (historians, anthropologists, critics, etc.) or laypeople on artists' styles, historical trends, or cultural traditions.
2. Students show their work in a simulated environment (such as a gallery opening, a courthouse trial, or a new museum exhibition) and judge the work of the other students based on the information researched.
3. Students role play and make comments on the work from the perspective of, for example, a particular artist, a critic, or a layperson.

This form of critique helps students to see historical and cultural relationships among works of art.

Art educators have long debated whether the arts should be subject to the types of assessment used in other school subjects. Some argue that the arts must be assessed in the same way as other subjects if people are to take the arts seriously and come to value them. Others argue that the important learning that takes place in art education cannot be assessed by such means because they actually trivialize the arts. However, in recent years, methods of assessment in the arts, such as portfolios and group critiques, have led assessment in other school subjects because they have held opportunities for assessing complex, higher-order types of learning to which conventional testing cannot provide access, such as imagination, critical thinking, and problem solving.

Although the arts have recently provided important alternative forms of assessment, such as performance methods, as models for general education, these methods have been used to continue the long-standing tradition of a focus on "the individual" in student achievement. This focus on individualism is an educational strength of art education because it fosters qualities of independent self-expression and esteem in student learning that can be important benefits of the arts. However, an extreme focus on individualism in art education can also be seen as a weakness because it promotes competitiveness in contrast to cooperation, ignores the importance of group identity, and detracts attention from the communal character of the creation of new knowledge.

GROUP COGNITION AND ASSESSMENT IN THE ARTS

A focus on individual assessment is consistent with the ideological structures that are foundations of capitalism and democracy, but at the same time, it confounds certain democratic ideals and attempts to cross cultural borders fairly. This perspective of individualism is reflected in the idea of genius as being innate and unrelated to sociocultural conditions, which has resulted in various forms of educational exclusion. Art curriculum has been shaped by such a conception of individualism through the interests of national agendas and beliefs about what is just in several ways. These include providing competitive vocational skills, nurturing certain (talented) individuals to the exclusion of others, and enabling therapeutic expression to overcome socially imposed pathologies and develop democratic personalities (Freedman, 1987).

As discussed in Chapter 4, theories of curriculum and assessment are designed in relation to models of child development and learning and these models are not neutral. They maintain certain beliefs about the growth of individuals in relation to society which have emerged through a particular cultural history. In democratic societies, the individual is focused upon as the manifestation of human rights and possibilities; but it can be argued that "the individual" existing in isolation from the realities of social environment is a somewhat mythical being. Until recently, Western models of child development and learning have been heavily defined in relation to this notion of individualism. Now, changing conditions, such as the international influence of Vygotsky in educational psychology and new interpretations of the work of Piaget and Dewey have placed the importance of social interaction to learning at the leading edge of curriculum studies.

Individual assessment is, of course, important, but it does have limitations. For example, all forms of assessment define knowledge as they reflect it. The divergent thinking and experimentalism that students learn in American schooling, where individualism is an intended out-come, still tends to be undervalued in assessment. As a result, rather than learning to channel such energy in preparation for a productive and enriched life outside of school, students learn how to prepare for forms of assessment that are peculiar to school. This process leads students to believe that knowledge is either objective, universal, and existing "out there somewhere," waiting to be learned by individuals or subjective and relativistic in that each individual is unique, with his or her own version of knowledge that is as good as any other. Such conceptions of assessment in education do not merely describe ideas and practices; they actually work to shape the way people think about and practice education.

In art education, as in other school subjects, it is extremely important to relate change in curriculum to change in the professional field. Such change in international arts communities now includes growing attention to the social conditions of art. The crossing of cultural and historical borders, the construction of multiple and group identities, and the importance of contexts of production and appreciation that are reflected in postmodern art are all part of these changing conditions. As a result, issues of artist collaboration, the world art market, art as social statement, and audience group response are becoming increasingly important in curriculum (Efland, Freedman, & Stuhr, 1996). The transformation of arts education, and education in general, reflects the shift in interest from epistemology to ontology and a questioning of whether the assessment of an object really focuses on the reconstruction of a producer's knowledge (context of production) or the viewer/listener's response (context of appreciation). For example, the work of Kara Walker, illustrated in Figure 8.1, resulted in some anger in viewers about her use of historical African–American stereotypes, but when viewers found out that she was African American and was making a comment on her own past, viewer response changed and an understanding developed of her work as a profound challenge to those stereotypes. These new issues of curriculum should be reflected in student assessment.

The Relationship between Group Learning and Assessment

The promotion and assessment of learning can be accomplished through social interaction among students. For example, at the University of Minnesota, David and Roger Johnson have done substantial empirical research over many years with cooperative learning groups. For Johnson and Johnson (1996), seven principles of assessment and reporting are

Figure 8.1. Kara Walker, *The Means to an End . . . A Shadow Drama in Five Acts.* 1995. Etching, aquatint on paper.

Collection Walker Art Center, Minneapolis. T.B. Walker Acquistion Fund, 1996

essential for assessment of cooperative learning: (1) design an assessment plan that takes account of teaching and learning processes, outcomes, and educational settings; (2) use cooperative student groups in assessing; (3) do not use "pseudo" groups that involve "free riding," hostility, and other dysfunctional social behaviors; (4) use groups that function cooperatively which "are characterized by positive interdependence, individual accountability, face-to-face promotive interaction, the appropriate use of interpersonal and small-group skills, and group processing" (pp. 25–26); (5) integrate assessment practices into instruction; (6) involve students in reporting assessment results; (7) use cooperative groups to help students individualize instructional and assessment goals and procedures.

Fundamentally, the plan described by Johnson and Johnson (1996) should help students focus on assessing and improving individual and group processes of learning, as well as assessing content outcomes. Truly cooperative groups should provide educational advantages for all students. The types of groups that are least effective are those assessed by a rank ordering within the group (resulting in competing and dishonest behaviors). Also of concern are groups made to work together, but with few joint responsibilities (such as assignments). In such situations, the more conscientious students may actually achieve more by working alone. Cooperative learning groups should work together to achieve shared goals, one of which is to promote the learning of all of the individuals in the group. As a result, Johnson and Johnson recommend criterion-referenced assessments and the continual checking of both individual and group progress.

Cooperative learning groups can be *formal* (lasting up to several weeks), *informal* (short term or ad hoc), or act as *base groups* (lasting at least a year) (Johnson & Johnson, 1996). However, essential to successful cooperative learning are the five elements that Johnson and Johnson have delineated after years of study. First, positive interdependence must be established so that students know they will either fail or succeed together; in other words, they are responsible for each other and the learning of each will benefit all. This can be established through common goals, rewards, and resources, as well as assessment criteria. Second, individual and group accountability are *both* important and interact. The group should make each individual learn more than each could alone. Third, promotive interaction, especially face-to-face encounters in which students do real work together, is important to strengthen ties, help them act as community, and promote each other's success. Fourth, social skills are considered part of curriculum and assessment. Students must be overtly taught such skills as leadership, negotiation, and conflict management. Fifth, group processing that in-volves group reflections on progress is fundamental to assessment. This includes considerations of ways the group can work more effectively together in order to meet academic goals.

Blumfeld, Marx, Soloway, and Krajcik (1996) support the Johnsons' argument that group learning should result in group, as well as in-dividual, assessment. They stress the importance of teacher under-standing of the processes that promote group learning and that group assessment should be part of the learning process. They state, "Effec-tive group work requires that students share ideas, take risks, disagree with and listen to others, and generate and reconcile points of view" (p. 38). As a result, the types of tasks given to students, conditions of giving and seeking help, individual accountability, and group compo-sition are important considerations in teacher planning. The promotion of collaboration is an essential element for success because it involves students in constructing shared meanings that will aid their understand-ing of disciplines and discipline communities.

Technological support for such collaboration could help to integrate group learning and assessment processes (e.g., Blumfeld et al., 1996; Freedman, 1989; Freedman & Liu, 1996). One reason for this is that technology can be used to keep a record of group interactions and the processes used in the creation of group products. These, then, can be-come part of student assessment. For example, in a study by Freedman and Liu (1996), three cultural groups of middle school students in vi-sual art, creative writing, and social studies classes in different states in the United States communicated with each other using the Internet. The students used this form of communication to study the other stu-dents' cultures. The knowledge that developed as a result of this con-tact was used as a foundation for student art and writing. The records of daily, casual correspondence, computer graphic image development, and formal peer review were kept on the computer and used as part of the assessment process.

One of the important aspects of arguments in favor of cooperative learning in school is that it shifts responsibility for student learning to the students themselves. This is particularly of interest now as the tech-nological mediation of learning is increasing through the use of com-puters and international mass media. In art education, this approach is reflected by classroom uses of technology where students may be taught to create their own curriculum on the web, network with students around the world, and recycle images created by others with ease and incredible speed. However, student responses to art are also an important part of learning and assessment. Students' ability to criticize their art and the work of others is a vital consideration in group assessment. Students should be able to take part in group critiques of individual student work, respond to group learning as a group, and respond as a group to professional artistic production and performance.

Fundamental to students taking increased responsibility for their own learning, and to several types of group forms of assessment, are student peer and self-assessment. If students are to monitor group activities in-process and be, at least in part, responsible for the success of the group, they must be taught how to analyze constructively and improve their own work and the work of others. Research has suggested that students who take part in self-assessment activities learn more about the arts than those who do not (Carole, 1995). However, self-assessment does not come easily, particularly in a competitive environment such as schooling. In order for students to take part in their own assessment, an education in assessment of the arts is required.

Assessment Communities

An important part of art education is its communal aspects. Communities for assessment can be seen on several levels, ranging from the professional arts communities that decide what is avant-garde to teaching communities that determine quality in student art. As Boughton (1997; Boughton, Eisner, & Ligtvoet, 1996) argues, communities of teachers function as arbiters of quality and can maintain or change conceptions of quality through debate and agreement. This interaction should be reflected in assessments of student groups and modeled for students to help them come to understand the role of social interaction in the formation of judgment.

Teachers' judgments about student art are rarely lacking in solid foundation. Quite the contrary, they are usually based on substantial tacit knowledge gained through study and experience. It is the character of the arts that makes this difficult for those outside the arts to understand. What teachers often lack is a way to articulate the knowledge on which they base their judgments. Boughton's (1997) argument for improving this situation stems from his experiences in countries outside the United States where groups of teachers have successfully validated their assessments, not by allowing governmental testing agencies to institute standardized forms of testing, but by working together to form communities that arbitrate the quality of student work. This process of peer review of teachers' judgments is called moderation.

Much of the discussion in this chapter is directed toward improving formative assessments, which are of the greatest education value. However, there is a need in the United States for reform of high-stakes assessment and national assessment surveys to reflect more appropriate methods for the arts and visual culture. In other countries, and the International Baccalaureate, consensual methods are more common.

STUDENT GROUP ASSESSMENT

Group forms of production and appreciation have long been traditions in the visual arts. Group forms of critique have also long been an established activity of the visual arts community. However, the literature discussed above suggests a range of new possibilities for the development of procedures through which groups of students can assess works of art. Through these procedures, students can discuss, debate, and judge the quality of learned concepts and skills.

Several aspects of group assessment are similar to those of individual assessment. For example, reflections of student imagination and the relationship of student production to lesson objectives are important to both. However, some aspects of group assessment are different, and involve changes in lesson design to accommodate, and even enhance, student collaboration and peer assessment. Such changes require a shift in thinking about the responsibilities of students for their own learning and the learning of their peers. This means that students must be made increasingly aware of the social conditions that enable, nurture, and limit judgments about quality in the arts.

Group methods of assessment are particularly important in the assessment of group works of art. As students develop social knowledge about the visual arts in the process of making or viewing group forms of art, they can begin to understand the relationship between their knowledge and its social value through group forms of assessment. Group works of art, including, for example, those of fine artists who work in pairs, television programmers and advertisers, and filmmakers, are highly complex and are assessed on multiple levels by many people. Group assessment of public visual arts occurs even when fine art, television, and film critics work alone in their authoring of criticism because even these individual efforts are part of a discourse community.

Three components of assessment are of particular importance when attending to the development of group forms of student assessment:

methods of procedure, methods of analysis, and *analysis criteria.* Methods of procedure are the ways in which evidence of performance and achievement is gathered, such as checklists, observations, or portfolios. Methods of analysis refer to the means by which decisions are made about the evidence and can be quantitative or qualitative. For example, a checklist usually leads to a quantitative analysis involving counting (for example, the number of techniques used by a student), whereas observation notes (which can be analyzed numerically, such as through a count of social interactions between students) provide opportunities for qualitative analysis involving an interpretation of student dialogue. The analysis criteria should determine the appropriate methods of procedure and analysis. In other words, as is the case with individual assessment, the way in which group assessment should be done is dependent on the goals of instruction.

Collaborative Forms of Portfolio Assessment

Wolf (1988–1989) describes a portfolio as "a chronologically sequenced collection of work that records the long-term evolution of artistic thinking" (p. 27). Portfolios have historically been used for individual student assessment in the arts. Generations of art students have enjoyed the type of individualized criticism that these portfolio assessments can help to provide.

> [In terms of] using portfolios for assessment of students, as self-directed learners, [they are] viewed through a wide lens in which [students] can be observed taking risks, solving problems creatively, and learning to judge their own performance and that of others. (Zimmerman, 1992, p. 17)

Similar types of portfolios used for individual assessment can be used to facilitate group assessment, including a portfolio that can reflect the best of the work of the students as a whole (Robinson, 1995). The procedures for developing and analyzing group portfolios can be the same as for individual portfolios. Several types of evidence should be included, such as examples of work and information about the work. In the visual arts, this involves examples of works of art, records of production processes, and student reflections about the art, including sketchbook and journal entries. Group portfolios can be developed in the same way for the production of group art and, at the same time, provide evidence of individual accountability and contribution. Group portfolios can also be used to assess group responses to professional art or the work of other groups of students.

Many group activities that support student learning, but may not directly result in the production or performance of art, can be assessed through the use of portfolios. For example, teaching-back (Snow, 1989), which involves students teaching peers what they have learned, can be documented using evidence of lesson planning.

Observation and Videotaping

Observing and recording group learning is an important part of teacher-based group assessment. These components of group assessment facilitate the analysis of social interaction, which, as we have seen, should be considered part of the learning objectives in group work. Students' performance, cooperation with others, work habits, and so on can be recorded using checklists, rubrics, and anecdotal descriptions.

Videotaping is a particularly powerful assessment tool in the arts. It is a concrete record of words, actions, and sounds, can be viewed repeatedly to allow for reflection and analysis, and it enables students to watch and critique themselves (e.g., Carlin, 1996; Zimmerman, 1992). For formative assessment, teachers might tape the production process of a group making a work of visual art or students may choose what and when to videotape. For example, they may wish to record a particularly difficult performance so that they can analyze it. For summative assessment, public performances and exhibitions can be taped and can include student commentary.

The difficulty with this method of procedure is to develop careful methods of analysis. Several questions should be addressed for an effective strategy: How will the observation/recording be done? What will be assessed? What social interactions illustrate student learning? Will the analysis be qualitative or quantitative? And so on.

Summary of Group Assessment Issues

The important points from the review and analysis of literature surrounding the topic of group assessment in the arts are highlighted in the following:

1. Individual assessment is important, but learning may be limited in focus and characterized by competition, exclusion, and social isolation.

2. Group assessment in arts education reflects the recent attention to the importance of collaboration and community in the arts.
3. Group assessment is consistent with empirical research that suggests the educational importance of socially shared cognition and cooperative learning.
4. Group assessment can reflect group learning and help students take responsibility for their own learning.
5. Individual accountability should be maintained as a part of group assessment.
6. Self and peer assessment is fundamental to successful group assessment.
7. The analysis of students' ability to work as a group and conduct self and peer assessment is essential for effective group assessment.
8. Group assessment can be done with formal, informal, or base groups.
9. Any group assessment plan must include predefined methods of procedure, methods of analysis, and analysis criteria.
10. Ways of gathering evidence include portfolios, observations, videotaping, and peer and self-critique.

In sum, three central issues are of particular importance in group forms of assessment. First, determining students' abilities to work in group contexts should be an essential part of any group assessment. Second, group assessment should include measures of individual accountability. Third, measures of individual accountability should include evidence of reflection on self and peer performance.

CONCLUSION

Studio production is vital to helping students understand the visual arts. It is the creation of unique images and objects, the freedom of making a statement, enrichment gained through the investigation of visual media, and the power of symbols to communicate that enable students to go reach outside of themselves, going beyond consumption and appropriation to become contributing members of larger communities and cultures. Although studying visual culture through various visual and textual processes are all helpful, making art is the surest way for students to come to understand the most fundamental reasons that visual culture is valuable enough to be taught in school: it is a way of knowing.

Assessing what students come to know about art through their studio work is often difficult and complex without the aid of a wide variety of visual experience and debate within communities. Experience should include a focus on the most up-to-date student and professional art being produced at any given time. And community debate must include continual challenge so that student art that goes beyond the hopes stated in instructional objectives, is rewarded.

References

Adorno, T. (1992). Letter to Walter Benjamin, March 18. In H. Zohn (Ed. & Trans.), *Aesthetics and politics* (pp. 120–126). London: New Left Books. Reprinted in F. Frascina & J. Harris (Eds.), *Art and modern culture* (pp. 74–75). New York: The Open University. (Original work published 1936)

Alexander, K. (1988). *Learning to look and create: The SPECTRA program*. Palo Alto, CA: Dale Seymour.

Anderson, J. (1980). *Cognitive psychology and its implications*. New York: W. H. Freeman.

Anderson, R. L. (1990). *Calliope's sisters: A comparative study of philosophies of art*. Englewood Cliffs, NJ: Prentice Hall.

Anderson, T. (1988). A structure for pedagogical art criticism. *Studies in Art Education, 30*(1), 28–38.

Anderson, T. (1993). Defining and structuring art criticism for education. *Studies in Art Education, 34*(4), 199–208.

Apple, M. W. (1972). Community, knowledge, and the structure of disciplines. *Educational Forum, 37*(1), 72–82.

Apple, M. W. (1975). The hidden curriculum and the nature of conflict. In W. Pinar (Ed.), *Curriculum theorizing: The reconceptualists* (pp. 95–119). Berkeley, CA: McCutchan.

Apple, M. W. (1986). *Teachers and texts: A political economy of class and gender relations in education*. New York: Routledge.

Aries, P. (1962). *Centuries of childhood*. London: Jonathan Cape.

Arnheim, R. (1974). *Art and visual perception: A psychology of the creative eye*. Berkeley: University of California Press.

Aronowitz, S. (1988). *Science as power discourse and ideology in modern society*. Minneapolis: University of Minnesota Press.

Baars, B. J. (1986). *The cognitive revolution in psychology*. New York: Guilford.

Barnard, M. (1995). Advertising: The rhetorical imperative. In C. Jencks (Ed.), *Visual culture* (pp. 26–41). London: Routledge.

Barnes, E. (1908). Child study in relation to elementary art education. In J. Haney (Ed.), *Art education in the United States* (pp. 101–132). New York: American Art Annual.

169

Barrett, T. (1990). *Criticizing photographs: An introduction to understanding images*. Mountain View, CA: Mayfield.

Barthes, R. (1974). *S/Z. English*. New York: Hill & Wang.

Baudrillard, J. (1983). *Simulations*. New York: Semiotext(e), Inc.

Bauman, Z. (1993). *Postmodern ethics*. Oxford, UK: Blackwell.

Beach, R., & Freedman, K. (1992). Responding as a cultural act: Adolescents' responses to magazine ads and short stories. In J. Many & C. Cox (Eds.), *Reader stance and literary understanding: Exploring the theories, research, and practice* (pp. 162–188). Norwood, NJ: Ablex.

Bell, C. (1913). *Art*. New York: Frederik A. Stokes Co.

Berenson, B. (1902). *The study and criticism of Italian art; Second series*. London: George Bell & Sons.

Berger, P., & Luckmann, T. (1967). *The social construction of reality*. Garden City, NY: Doubleday.

Bernstein, R. (1986). The rage against reason. *Philosophy and Literature, 10*(2), 186–210.

Best, S., & Kellner, D. (1991). *Postmodern theory: Critical interrogations*. New York: Guilford.

Beyer, L., & Liston, D. P. (1996). *Curriculum in conflict: Social vision, educational agendas, and progressive school reform*. New York: Teachers College Press.

Blandy, D. (1994). Assuming responsibility: Disability rights and the preparation of art teachers. *Studies in Art Education, 35*(3), 179–187.

Blumfeld, P. C., Marx, R. W., Soloway, E., & Krajcik, J. (1996). Learning with peers: From small group cooperation to collaborative communities. *Educational Researcher, 25*(8), 37–40.

Blumler, J. G. (1992). *The future of children's television in Britain: An enquiry for the Broadcasting Standards Council*. London: Broadcasting Standards Council.

Boden, M. A. (1992). *The creative mind: Myths and mechanics*. New York: Basic Books.

Bogart, L. (1956). *The age of television: A study of viewing habits and the impact of television on American life*. New York: Frederick Ungar.

Bogart, M. H. (1995). *Artists, advertising, and the borders of art*. Chicago: University of Chicago Press.

Botta, R. (2000). The mirror of television: A comparison of black and white adolescents' body image. *Journal of Communication, 32*(1), 6–16.

Boughton, D. (1994). *Evaluation and assessment in visual arts education*. Geelong, Victoria, Australia: Deakin University.

Boughton, D. (1996). Assessment of student learning in the visual arts. *Translations from Theory to Practice, 6*(3), National Art Education Association.

Boughton, D. (1997). Reconsidering issues of assessment and achievement standards in art education. *Studies in Art Education, 38*(4), 199–213.

Boughton, D., Eisner, E., & Ligtvoet, J. (1996). *Evaluating and assessing the visual arts in education: International perspectives*. New York: Teachers College Press.

Bourdieu, P. (1984). *Distinction: A social critique of the judgment of taste* (R. Nice, Trans.). Cambridge, MA: Harvard University Press.

Bourdieu, P. (1993). *The field of cultural production.* London: Polity Press.

Braudel, F. (1980). *On history* (S. Matthews, Trans.). Chicago: University of Chicago Press. (Original work published 1969)

Brett, G. (1987). *Through our own eyes: Popular art and modern history.* London: GMP.

Brittain, W. L. (1990). Children's drawings: A comparison of two cultures. In B. Young (Ed.) *Art, culture, and ethnicity* (pp. 181–192). Reston, VA: NAEA. (Reprinted from *Journal of Multicultural and Cross-cultural Research in Art Education,* Fall 1985.)

Broudy, H. A. (1972). *Enlightened cherishing: An essay on aesthetic education.* Urbana, IL, Chicago, London: University of Illinois Press.

Broudy, H. A. (1987). *The role of imagery in learning.* Los Angeles, CA: Getty Center for Education in the Arts.

Brownell, C., & Carriger, M. (1991). Collaborations among toddler peers: Individual contributions to social contexts. In L. Resnick, J. Levine, & S. Teasley (Eds.), *Perspectives on socially shared cognition* (pp. 365–383). Washington, DC: American Psychological Association.

Bryson, N. (1983). *Vision and painting: The logic of the gaze.* New Haven, CT: Yale University Press.

Canada, K., & Brusca, F. (1991). The technological gender gap: Evidence and recommendations for educators and computer-based instruction designers. *Educational Technology Research and Development, 39*(2), 43–51.

Carlin, J. (1996). Videotape as an assessment tool. *Teaching Music, 3*(4), 38–39, 54.

Carole, P. J. (1995). Alternative assessment in music education. Unpublished masters thesis, Nova Southeastern University. East Lansing, MI: National Center for Research on Teacher Learning. (ERIC Document Service No. ED 398 141) (Report no. 50 026 723)

Castiglione, L. V. (1996). Portfolio assessment in art and education. *Art Education Policy Review, 97,* 2–9.

Chalmers, F. G. (1981). Art education as ethnology. *Studies in Art Education, 22*(3), 6–14.

Champagne, A. B., Klopfer, L. E., & Anderson, J. H. (1980). Factors influencing the learning of classical mechanics. *American Journal of Physics, 48,* 174.

Chapman, L. H. (1987). *Discover art: Grade 2.* Worcester, MA: Davis.

Cherryholmes, C. H. (1988). *Power and criticism.* New York: Teachers College Press.

Clifford, J. (1988). *The predicament of culture: Twentieth century ethnography, literature, and art.* Cambridge, MA: Harvard University Press.

Cole, M., & Engestrom, Y. (1993). A cultural-historical approach to distributed cognition. In G. Salomon (Ed.), *Distributed cognition: Psychological and educational considerations* (pp. 1–46). New York: Cambridge University Press.

Congdon, K. G. (1989). Multi-cultural approaches to art criticism. *Studies in Art Education, 30*(3), 176–184.

Coote, J., & Shelton, A. (Eds.). (1992). *Anthropology, art and aesthetics.* Oxford, UK: Clarendon Press.

Cox, M. V. (1993). *Children's drawings of the human figure.* Hove, UK: Erlbaum.

Crowther, P. (1993). *Critical aesthetics and postmodernism.* Oxford, UK: Clarendon

Dahl, R. A. (1971). *Polyarchy: Participation and opposition.* New Haven, CT: Yale University Press.

de Lauretis, T. (1987). *Technologies of gender: Essays on theory, film, and fiction.* Bloomington: Indiana University Press.

Derrida, J. (1976). *Of gramotology.* Baltimore: Johns Hopkins University Press.

DeVillar, R. A., & Faltis, C. J. (1991). *Computers and cultural diversity: Restructuring for school success.* Albany, NY: SUNY Press.

Dewey, J. (1944). *Democracy and education: An introduction to the philosophy of education.* New York: Free Press. (Original work published 1916)

Dewey, J. (1934). *Art as experience.* New York: Capricorn Books.

Diem, R. A. (1986). Computers in a school environment: Preliminary report of the social consequences. *Theory and Research in Social Education, 14*(2), 163–170.

Doll, W. (1993). *A post-modern perspective on curriculum.* New York: Teachers College Press.

Douglas, A. (1977). *The feminization of American culture.* New York: Doubleday.

Duncum, P. (1984). How 35 children born between 1724 and 1900 learned to draw. *Studies in Art Education, 26*(2), 93–102.

Duncum, P. (1988). To copy or not to copy: A review. *Studies in Art Education, 29*(4), 203–210.

Duncum, P. (1989). Children's unsolicited drawings of violence as a site of social contradiction. *Studies in Art Education, 30*(4), 249–256.

Duncum, P. (1990). Clearing the decks for dominant culture: Some first principles for a contemporary art education. *Studies in Art Education, 31*(4), 207–215.

During, S. (Ed.). (1993). *The cultural studies reader.* London: Routledge.

Durkin, K. (1985). *Television, sex-roles, and children.* Milton Keynes, UK: Open University Press.

Eagleton, T. (1983). *Literary theory: An introduction.* Minneapolis: University of Minnesota Press.

Edwards, S. (Ed.). (1998). *Art and its histories.* New Haven, CT: Yale University Press.

Efland, A. (1976). School art style: A functional analysis. *Studies in Art Education, 17*(2), 37–44.

Efland, A., Freedman, K., & Stuhr, P. (1996). *Postmodern art education: An approach to curriculum.* Reston, VA: NAEA.

Ehman, L. E., Glenn, A. D., Johnson, V., & White, C. S. (1992). Using computer databases in student problem solving: A study of eight social studies teachers' classrooms. *Theory and Research in Social Education, 20*(2), 179–206.

Eisner, E. W. (1973/1974). Does behavioral objective and accountability have a place in art education? *Art Education, 26*(5), 2–5. Reprinted in G. W. Hardiman & T. Zernich (Eds.), *Curricular considerations for visual arts education: Rationale, development, and evaluation* (pp. 185–194). Champaign, IL: Stipes.

Eisner, E. W. (1979). *The educational imagination: On the design and evaluation of school programs.* New York: Macmillan.

Eisner, E. W. (1982). *Cognition and curriculum: A basis for deciding what to teach.* New York: Longman.

Eisner, E. W. (1985).*The educational imagination: On the design and evaluation of school programs.* New York: Macmillan.

Eisner, E. W. (1998). *The kind of schools we need: Personal essays.* Portsmouth, NH: Heinemann.

Encounters (2000). *Exhibition catalogue.* Edinburgh: Scottish Museum of Art.

Engle, S. (1960). Decision making. *Social Education, 24,* 301–306.

Erickson, M. A. (1994). Evidence for art historical interpretation referred to by young people and adults. *Studies in Art Education, 35*(2), 71–78.

Erickson, M. A. (1998). Effects of art history instruction on fourth and eighth grade students' abilities to interpret artworks contextually. *Studies in Art Education, 39*(4), 309–320.

Ewen, S. (1988). *All consuming images: The politics of style in contemporary culture.* New York: Basic Books.

Feldman, E. B. (1967). *Art as image and idea.* Englewood Cliffs, NJ: Prentice-Hall.

Feldman, E. B. (1970). *Becoming human through art.* Englewood Cliffs, NJ: Prentice-Hall.

Fish, S. (1982). *Is there a text in this class: The authority of interpretive communities.* Cambridge, MA: Harvard University Press.

Fosnot, C. T. (1996). Constructivism: A psychological theory of learning. In C. T. Fosnot (Ed.), *Constructivism: Theory, perspectives, and practice* (pp. 8–33). New York: Teachers College Press.

Foucault, M. (1970). *The order of things: An archaeology of the human sciences* (Trans. of *Les mots et les choses,* 1966). New York: Vintage Books.

Freedberg, D. (1989). *The power of images: Studies in the history and theory of response.* Chicago: University of Chicago Press.

Freedman, K. (1987). Art education and changing political agendas: An analysis of curriculum concerns of the 1940s and 1950s. *Studies in Art Education, 29*(1), 17–29.

Freedman, K. (1989). Microcomputers and the dynamics of image making and social life in three art classrooms. *Journal of Research on Computing in Education, 21*(3), 290–298.

Freedman, K. (1991). Possibilities of interactive computer graphics for art instruction: A summary of research. *Art Education, 44*(3), 41–47.

Freedman, K. (1992). Structure and transformation in art education: The Enlightenment project and the institutionalization of nature. In D. Thistlewood (Ed.), *Studies in the History of Art and Design Education*. London: Longman Press.

Freedman, K. (1994). Interpreting gender and visual culture in art classrooms. *Studies in Art Education, 35*(3), 157–170.

Freedman, K. (1995). Educational change within structures of history, culture, and discourse. In R. W. Neperud (Ed.), *Context, content, and community in art education* (pp. 87–107). New York: Teachers College Press.

Freedman, K. (1997a). Artistic development and curriculum: Sociocultural considerations. In A. M. Kindler (Ed.), *Child Development in Art* (pp. 95–106). Reston, VA: NAEA.

Freedman, K. (1997b). Representations of fine art in popular culture: Curriculum inside and outside of school. *Journal of Art and Design Education, 16*(2), 137–146.

Freedman, K. (2000). Social perspectives on art education in the U.S.: Teaching visual culture in a democracy. *Studies in Art Education. 41*(4), 314–329.

Freedman, K., & Liu, M. (1996). The importance of computer experience, learning processes, and communication patterns in multicultural networking. *Educational Technology Research and Development, 44*(1), 43–60.

Freedman, K., & Relan, A. (1992). Computer graphics, artistic production and social processes. *Studies in Art Education, 33*(2), 98–109.

Freedman, K., & Wood, J. (1999). Student knowledge of visual culture: Images inside and outside of school. *Studies in Art Education, 2*(40), 128–142.

Furnham, A., & Stacey, B. (1991). *Young people's understanding of society.* London: Routledge.

Garber, E. (1990). Implications of feminist art criticism for art education. *Studies in Art Education, 32*(1), 17–26.

Garber, E. (1995). Teaching art in the context of culture: A study in the borderlands. *Studies in Art Education, 36*(4), 218–232.

Gardner, H. (1991). *The unschooled mind: How children think and how schools should teach.* New York: Basic Books.

Gardner, H., Winner, E., & Kirchner, M. (1975). Children's conceptions of the arts. *Journal of Aesthetic Education, 9*(3), 61–77.

Gelman, S. A., Coley, J. D., & Gottfried, G. M. (1994). Essentialist beliefs in children: The acquisition of concepts and theories. In L. A. Hirschfeld & S. A. Gelman (Eds.), *Mapping the mind: Domain specificity in cognition and culture.* Cambridge, UK: Cambridge University Press.

Gessell, A. (1940). *The first five years of life: A guide to the study of the preschool child.* New York: Harper & Brothers.

Giroux, H. A. (1992). *Border crossings: Cultural workers and the politics of education.* New York: Routledge.

Giroux, H. A. (1994). *Disturbing pleasures: Learning popular culture.* New York: Routledge.

Giroux, H. A., & Simon, R. I. (1989). *Popular culture: Schooling and everyday life.* Granby, MA: Bergin & Garvey.

Goffman, E. (1979). *Gender advertisements*. New York: Harper & Row.

Golomb, C. (1974). *Young children's sculpture and drawing: A study in representational development*. Cambridge, MA: Harvard University Press.

Gombrich, E. H. (1966). Norm & form: The stylistic categories of art history and their origins in Renaissance ideals (pp. 83–94). In *Norm & form: Studies in the art of the Renaissance* (vol. 1). London: Phaidon. Reprinted in Edwards, S. (Ed.), *Art and its histories: A reader*. New Haven, CT: Yale University Press.

Gormally, M. F., & Nunn, P. G. (1988). Teaching and learning. In A. L. Rees & F. Borzello (Eds.), *The new art history* (pp. 55–62). Atlantic Highlands, NJ: Humanities Press.

Graff, G. (1987). *Professing literature: An institutional history*. Chicago: University of Chicago Press.

Greenberg, C. (1959). Avant-garde and kitsch. In B. Rosenberg & D. M. White (Eds.), *Mass culture: The popular arts in America* (pp. 98–111). Glencoe, IL: The Free Press. (Reprinted from *The Partisan Reader*, 1946, pp. 378–389.)

Greenfield, P. M. (1984). *Mind and media: The effects of television, video games, and computers*. Cambridge, MA: Harvard University Press.

Griffin, A. (1996). Teaching in authoritarian and democratic states. In W. C. Parker (Ed.), *Educating the democratic mind* (pp. 79–94). Albany: SUNY Press.

Grossberg, L., Nelson, C., & Treichler, P. (Eds.). (1992). *Cultural studies*. New York: Routledge.

Guilbaud, S. (1984). *How New York stole the idea of modern art: Abstract Expressionism, freedom, and the Cold War*. Chicago: University of Chicago Press.

Habermas, J. (1976). *Legitimation crisis*. Boston: Beacon Press.

Habermas, J. (1987). *The philosophical discourse of modernity* (F. Lawrence, Trans.). Cambridge, UK: Cambridge University Press.

Hall, G. S. (1911). *Educational problems* (Vol. 2). New York: D. Appleton.

Harvey, D. (1989). *The condition of postmodernity: An enquiry into the origins of cultural change*. Oxford, UK: Basil Blackwell.

Hauser, A. (1982). *The sociology of art* (K. J. Northcott, Trans.). Chicago: University of Chicago Press. (Original work published 1974)

Hauser, A. (1985). *The social history of art*. New York: Vintage Books.

Hein, H. (1993). *Aesthetics in feminist perspective*. Bloomington: Indiana University Press.

Hicks, L. E. (1990). A feminist analysis of empowerment and community in art education. *Studies in Art Education, 32*(1), 36–46.

Hughes, R. (1999, February 8). Wynn win? *Time*, 49–53.

Jackson, P. (1968). *Life in classrooms*. New York: Holt, Rinehart & Winston.

Jameson, F. (1984). Postmodernism, or the logic of late capitalism. *New Left Review, 146*, 53–92.

Jameson, F. (1991). *Postmodernism, or the logic of late capitalism*. Durham, NC: Duke University Press.

Jauss, H. R. (1982). *Toward an aesthetic of reception* (T. Bahti, Trans.). Minneapolis: University of Minnesota Press.

Johnson, D. W. , & Johnson, R. T. (1996). The role of cooperative learning in assessing and communicating student learning. In T. T. Guskey (Ed.), *Communicating student learning* (pp. 25–46). Alexandria, VA: ASCD Yearbook.

Johnson, R. T., Johnson, D. W., & Stanne, M. B. (1986). Comparison of computer-assisted cooperative, competitive, and individualistic learning. *American Educational Research Journal, 23*(3), 382–392.

Jordanova, L. J. (1980). Natural facts: A historical perspective on science and sexuality. In C. MacCormick & M. Strathern (Eds.). *Nature, culture and gender* (pp. 42–69). Cambridge, UK: Cambridge University Press.

Joshua, S., & Dupin, J. J. (1987). Taking into account students conceptions in a didactic strategy: An example in physics. *Cognition and Instruction, 4*, 117–135.

Joyce, B., & Weil, M. (1986). *Models of teaching*. Englewood, NJ: Prentice-Hall.

Kearney, R. (1988). *The wake of imagination: Towards a postmodern culture*. Minneapolis: University of Minnesota Press.

Kellogg, R. (1969). *Analyzing children's art*. Palo Alto, CA: Mayfield.

Kershensteiner, G. (1905). *Die entwicklung der zeichnerischen begabung* (Development of a graphic gift). Munich: Carl Gerber.

Kincheloe, J. L., & Steinberg, S. R. (1993). A tentative description of post-formal thinking: The critical confrontation with cognitive theory. *Harvard Educational Review, 63*(3), 296–320.

Kindler, A. M. (1994). Children and the culture of a multicultural society. *Art Education, 47*(4), 54–60.

Kindler, A. M. (Ed.). (1997). *Child development in art*. Reston, VA: NAEA.

Kindler, A. M. (1999). "From endpoints to repertoires": A challenge to art education. *Studies in Art Education, 40*(4), 330–340.

Kohlberg, L. (1981). *Essays on moral development*. San Francisco: Harper & Row.

Koroscik, J. (1990). Novice-expert differences in understanding and misunderstanding art and their implications for student assessment in art education. *Art and Learning Research, 8*, 6–29.

Krauss, R. M. , & Fussell, S. R. (1991). Constructing shared communicative environments. In L. B. Resnick, J. M. Levine, & S. D. Teasley (Eds.), *Perspectives of socially shared cognition* (pp. 63–82). Washington, DC: American Psychological Association.

Lacan, J. (1977). *The four fundamental concepts of psycho-analysis*. London: Penguin.

Langley, P., & Simon, H. A. (1981). The central learning in cognition. In J. R. Anderson (Ed.), *Cognitive skills and their acquisition* (pp. 361–380). Hillsdale, NJ: Erlbaum.

Lanier, V. (1969). The teaching of art as social revolution. *Phi Delta Kappan, 50*(6), 314–319.

Larkin, J. (1981). Enriching formal knowledge: A model for learning to solve textbook physics problems. In J. R. Anderson (Ed.), *Cognitive skills and their acquisition* (pp. 311–334). Hillsdale, NJ: Erlbaum.

Lave, J. (1991). Situated learning in communities of practice. In L. B. Resnick, J. M. Levine, & S. D. Teasley (Eds.), *Perspectives of socially shared cognition* (pp. 63–82). Washington, DC: American Psychological Association.

Layton, R. (1991). *The anthropology of art* (2nd ed.). Cambridge, UK: Cambridge University Press.

Leland, J. (1999, August 16). *The Blair witch cult. Newsweek*, 44–49.

Leppert, R. (1996). *Art and the committed eye: Culture, society, and the cultural functions of imagery.* Boulder, CO: Westwood.

Leuthold, S. (1998). *Indigenous aesthetics: Native art and identity.* Austin: University of Texas Press.

Lichter, S. R., & Lichter, L. (1988, Spring). Does television shape ethnic images? *Media Values, 43,* 5–8.

Littlejohn, J. R. (1999, December 17). We the jury. *TV Guide,* 29–33.

Lowenfeld, V. (1947). *Creative and mental growth.* New York: Macmillan.

Lowenfeld, V. (1957). *Creative and mental growth* (3rd ed.). New York: Macmillan.

Lowenfeld, V., & Brittain, W. L. (1964). *Creative and mental growth* (4th ed.). New York: Macmillan.

Lowenthal, L. (1959). Historical perspectives of popular culture (pp. 46–73). In B. Rosenberg & D. M. White (Eds.), *Mass culture: The popular arts in America.* Glencoe, IL: Free Press. (Reprinted from *The American Journal of Sociology, 55,* 1950, pp. 323–332.)

Lucie-Smith, E. (1981). *The story of craft: The craftman's role in society.* Oxford, UK: Phaidon.

Lyotard, J. (1984). *The postmodern condition: A report on knowledge.* Minneapolis: University of Minnesota Press.

Marzano, R. J. (1992). *A different kind of classroom: Teaching with dimensions of learning.* Alexandria, VA: Association for Curriculum and Supervision.

McCormick, P. J. (1990). *Modernity, aesthetics, and the bounds of art.* Ithaca, NY: Cornell University Press.

McNeil, J. D. (1975). *Curriculum: A comprehensive introduction.* New York: Scott Foresman.

McNeil, J. D. (1996). *Curriculum: A comprehensive introduction* (5th ed.). Glenview, IL: Scott Foresman/Little, Brown Higher Education.

Mead, R. (1998, July 13). Rag trade. *New Yorker,* 25–26.

Morley, D. (1992). *Television, audiences, and cultural studies.* London: Routledge.

Muffoletto R., & Knupfer, N. N. (Eds.). (1993*). Computers and education: Social, political, and historical perspectives.* Cresskill, NJ: Hampton.

Neperud, R. W. (1988). Conceptions of art in the service of art and aesthetic education: A critical view. *Arts and Learning Research, 6,* 95–102.

Nodine, C., Locher, P., & Krupinski, E. (1993). The role of formal training on perception and aesthetic judgment of art compositions. *Leonardo, 26,* 219–227.

Norman, D. (1993). *Things that make us smart: Defending human attributes in the age of the machine.* Reading, MA: Perseus Books.

Novak, J. D. (1977). An alternative to Piagetian psychology for science and mathematics education. *Science Education, 61,* 453–477.

Oliver, D. W., & Shaver, J. P. (1966). *Teaching public issues in the high school.* Boston: Houghton Mifflin.

Paget, G. W. (1932). Some drawings of men and women made by children of certain non-European races. *Journal of the Royal Anthropological Institute, 62,* 127–144.

Palinscar, A. S., & Brown, A. L. (1984). Reciprocal teaching of comprehension-fostering and monitoring activities. *Cognition and Instruction, 1*(2), 117–175.

Parsons, M. J. (1987). *How we understand art: A cognitive development account of aesthetic experience.* Cambridge, UK: Cambridge University Press.

Pereira, L. (2000). An analysis of a high school art course. Unpublished manuscript.

Persky, H. R., Sandene, B. A., & Askew, J. M. (1998). *NAEP 1997 arts report card: Eighth grade findings from the national assessment of educational progress.* Washington, DC: NAEP.

Poster, M. (1994). The mode of information and postmodernity. In D. Crowley & D. Mitchell (Eds.), *Communication theory today* (pp. 173–192). Stanford, CA: Stanford University Press.

Prawat, R. S. (1989). Promoting access to knowledge, strategy, and disposition in students: A research synthesis. *Review of Educational Research, 59*(1), 1–41.

Prawat, R. S. (1996). Learning community, commitment, and school reform. *Journal of Curriculum Studies, 18*(1), 91–110.

Preziosi, D. (1989). *Rethinking art history: Meditations on a coy science.* New Haven, CT: Yale University Press.

Radway, J. (1985). *Reading the romance.* Chapel Hill, NC: University of North Carolina Press.

Resnick, L. B. (1987). Constructing knowledge in school. In L. S. Lisbon (Ed.), *Development and learning: Conflict or congruence* (pp. 19–50). Hillsdale, NJ: Erlbaum.

Resnick, L. B. (1994). Situated rationalism: Biological and social preparation for learning. In L. A. Hirschfeld & S. A. Gelman (Eds.), *Mapping the mind: Domain specificity in cognition and culture.* Cambridge, MA: Cambridge University Press.

Robinson, M. (1995). Alternative assessment techniques for teachers. *Music Educators Journal, 81*(5), 28–34.

Rosenberg, H. (1972). *The definition of art.* New York: Macmillan.

Rysavy, S. D. M., & Sales, G. C. (1991). Cooperative learning in computer-based instruction. *Educational Technology Research and Development, 39*(2), 70–80.

Schaefer-Simmern, H. (1950). *The unfolding of artistic ability*. Berkeley: University of California Press.

Schon, D. A. (1987). *Educating the reflective practitioner*. San Francisco: Jossey-Bass.

Schwartz, J. (1984). *The sexual politics of Jean-Jacques Rousseau*. Chicago: University of Chicago Press.

Sheets, H. M. (2000, September). Baffled, bewildered, and smitten: How to learn to stop worrying and love the art you don't understand. *Artnews*, 130.

Shepard, L. (2000). The role of assessment in a learning culture. *Educational Researcher, 29*(7), 4–14.

Short, G. (1998). The high school studio curriculum and art understanding: An examination. *Studies in Art Education, 40*(1), 46–65.

Shusterman, R. (1992). *Pragmatist aesthetics: Living beauty, rethinking art*. Oxford, UK: Blackwell.

Slattery, P. (1995). *Curriculum development in the postmodern era*. New York: Garland.

Sleeter, C. E., & Grant, C. (1987). An analysis of multicultural education in the United States. *Harvard Educational Review, 57*(4), 421–444.

Smith-Shank, D. (1993). Beyond this point there be dragons: Pre-service elementary teachers' stories of art and education. *Art Education, 46*(5), 45–51.

Smith-Shank, D. (1995). Semiotic pedagogy and art education. *Studies in Art Education, 36*(4), 233–241.

Smith-Shank, D. (1996). Microethnography of a Grateful Dead event: American subculture aesthetics. *Journal of Multicultural and Cross-cultural Research in Art Education, 14*, 80–91.

Snow, R. (1989). Toward assessment of cognitive and cognitive structures in learning. *Educational Researcher, 47*(7), 8–14.

Solso, R. (1994). *Cognition and the visual arts*. Cambridge, MA: MIT Press.

Solso, R. (1997). *Mind and brain sciences in the 21st century*. Cambridge, MA: MIT Press.

Sparke, P. (1995). *As long as it's pink: The sexual politics of taste*. London: HarperCollins.

Stuhr, P. (1991). Contemporary approaches to multicultural art education in the United States. *INSEA News, 1*, 14–15.

Stuhr, P. (1994). Multicultural art education and social reconstruction. *Studies in Art Education, 35*(3), 171–178.

Stuhr, P., Petrovich-Mwaniki, L., & Wasson, R. (1992). Curriculum guidelines for the multicultural classroom. *Art Education, 45*(1), 16–24.

Subcommittee on Curriculum of the Bureau of Education Committee of the International Kindergarten Union. (1919). *The kindergarten curriculum. Bulletin of the U.S. Bureau of Education, 16*. Washington, DC: U.S. Government Printing Office.

Sullivan, G. (1994). *Seeing Australia: Views of artists and artwriters*. Annandale, New South Wales, Australia: Piper Press.

Sully, J. (1895). *Studies of childhood*. New York: D. Appleton.

Szombati-Fabian, I., & Fabian, J. (1976). Art, history, and society: Popular painting in Shaba, Zaire. *Studies in the Anthropology of Visual Communication*, *3*(1), 1–21.

Taba, H., & Elzey, F. F. (1964). Teaching strategies and thought processes. *Teachers College Record*, *65*(6), 524–534.

Thompson, J. B. (1994). Social theory and the media. In D. Crowley & D. Mitchell (Eds.), *Communication theory today* (pp. 27–49). Stanford, CA: Stanford University Press.

Thorndike, E. L. (1913, November). The measurement of achievement in drawing. *Teachers College Record*, *14*, 345–382.

Tulloch, J., & Jenkins, H. (1995). *Science fiction audiences: Watching* Dr. Who *and* Star Trek. London: Routledge.

Vosniadou, S., & Brewer, W. F. (1987). Theories of knowledge restructuring in development. *Review of Educational Research*, *57*(1), 51–67.

Walkerdine, V. (1988). *The mastery of reason: Cognitive development and the production of rationality*. London: Routledge.

Wasson, R., Stuhr, P., & Petrovich-Mwaniki, L. (1990). Teaching art in the multicultural classroom: Six position statements. *Studies in Art Education*, *31*(4), 234–246.

Webb, N. M., & Palinscar, A. S. (1996). Group processes in the classroom. In D. C. Berliner & R. Calfee (Eds.), *Handbook of educational psychology* (pp. 841–873). New York: Macmillian.

Werckmeister, O. K. (1977). The issue of the child in the art of Paul Klee. *Arts Magazine*, *52*, 138–151.

Williamson, J. (1978). *Decoding advertisements: Ideology and meaning in advertising*. London: Marion Boyars.

Wilson, B., Hurwitz, A., & Wilson, M. (1987). *Teaching drawing from art*. Worchester, MA: Davis.

Wilson, B., & Wilson, M. (1977). An iconoclastic view of the imagery sources of the drawing of young people. *Art Education*, *30*(1), 5–11.

Wolf, D. P. (1988–1989). Opening up assessment. *Educational Leadership*, *45*(4), 24–29.

Wölfflin, H. (1950). *The principles of art history: The problem of the development of style in later art* (M. D. Hoffinger, Trans.). London: Dover. Reprinted in Edwards, S. (Ed.) *Art and its histories: A reader*. New Haven, CT: Yale University Press. (Original work published 1915)

Yarbus, A. L. (1967). *Eye movements and vision*. New York: Plenum.

Zimmerman, E. (1992). Assessing students' progress and achievements in art. *Art Education*, *45*(6), 14–24.

Index

About the Author

KERRY FREEDMAN is a professor of art and education at Northern Illinois University (NIU). She recently moved to NIU after teaching for 15 years at the University of Minnesota. She received her Ph.D. in curriculum and instruction in 1985 from the University of Wisconsin-Madison. She has taught art at all levels and has been teaching for over 25 years. Professor Freedman's research focuses on the relationship of curriculum to society and culture. Recently, she has concentrated on student engagement with visual culture and the postmodern conditions of education. Dr. Freedman has published extensively on art, education, and technology, including articles in *Studies in Art Education*, *Journal of Art and Design Education*, *Educational Technology Research and Development*, and the *Journal of Curriculum Studies*. She speaks regularly to regional, national, and international audiences. Professor Freedman has coauthored a book entitled *Postmodern Art Education: An Approach to Curriculum* and coedited the book *Curriculum, Culture, and Art Education* with Fernando Hernandez. She is on several editorial boards, including that of the British *Journal of Art and Design Education*, and is the senior editor of *Studies in Art Education*. Professor Freedman is a distinguished fellow of the National Art Education Association.